Cambridge Elements ≡

Elements in Philosophy and Logic
edited by
Bradley Armour-Garb
SUNY Albany
Frederick Kroon
The University of Auckland

PROBABILITY AND INDUCTIVE LOGIC

Antony Eagle
University of Adelaide

CAMBRIDGE
UNIVERSITY PRESS

CAMBRIDGE
UNIVERSITY PRESS

Shaftesbury Road, Cambridge CB2 8EA, United Kingdom

One Liberty Plaza, 20th Floor, New York, NY 10006, USA

477 Williamstown Road, Port Melbourne, VIC 3207, Australia

314–321, 3rd Floor, Plot 3, Splendor Forum, Jasola District Centre, New Delhi – 110025, India

103 Penang Road, #05–06/07, Visioncrest Commercial, Singapore 238467

Cambridge University Press is part of Cambridge University Press & Assessment, a department of the University of Cambridge.

We share the University's mission to contribute to society through the pursuit of education, learning and research at the highest international levels of excellence.

www.cambridge.org
Information on this title: www.cambridge.org/9781009507585

DOI: 10.1017/9781009210171

© Antony Eagle 2024

When citing this work, please include a reference to the DOI 10.1017/9781009210171

First published 2024

A catalogue record for this publication is available from the British Library.

ISBN 978-1-009-50758-5 Hardback
ISBN 978-1-009-21019-5 Paperback
ISSN 2516-418X (online)
ISSN 2516-4171 (print)

Additional resources for this publication at www.cambridge.org/Eagle

Probability and Inductive Logic

Elements in Philosophy and Logic

DOI: 10.1017/9781009210171
First published online: December 2024

Antony Eagle
University of Adelaide

Author for correspondence: Antony Eagle, antony.eagle@adelaide.edu.au

Abstract: Reasoning from inconclusive evidence, or 'induction', is central to science and any applications we make of it. For that reason alone it demands the attention of philosophers of science. This Element explores the prospects of using probability theory to provide an inductive logic: a framework for representing evidential support. Constraints on the ideal evaluation of hypotheses suggest that the overall standing of a hypothesis is represented by its probability in light of the total evidence, and incremental support, or confirmation, indicated by the hypothesis having a higher probability conditional on some evidence than it does unconditionally. This proposal is shown to have the capacity to reconstruct many canons of the scientific method and inductive inference. Along the way, significant objections are discussed, such as the challenge of inductive scepticism, and the objection that the probabilistic approach makes evidential support arbitrary.

Keywords: induction, Bayesian epistemology, confirmation theory, evidential support, prior probability

ISBNs: 9781009507585 (HB), 9781009210195 (PB), 9781009210171 (OC)
ISSNs: 2516-418X (online), 2516-4171 (print)

Contents

Introduction and Overview

To practice the intellectual virtue of open-mindedness, steering between the vices of fickleness and obstinacy, one must respond to evidence in a way that respects the *bearing of that evidence* on matters one is considering. This Element is about that notion. While deductive logic scaffolds the relationship between evidence and hypothesis, a full account – an *inductive logic* – will involve 'weighing evidence and judging probability' (Lipton 2004, p. 5).

In Section 1, I begin by distinguishing inductive inference from deductive logic and consider what the project of 'inductive logic' could be now (as opposed to various projects that historically went under that label). I propose that 'inductive logic' could serve as a good label for the study of relations of evidential support and confirmation. Reflection on Hume's venerable 'problem of induction', as well as some elementary considerations of the logic of confirmation, reveals some basic constraints any account must respect. Section 2 starts on the positive project, proposing to understand the degree to which a hypothesis is supported as relative to a particular ideal perspective on the hypothesis, given a background body of total evidence and a conception of evidential support. It is there argued that these epistemic perspectives must have a probabilistic structure and that they are not necessarily to be identified with the actual attitudes of any individual. Thus the account on offer is broadly Bayesian, yet not wholly subjectivist. Having introduced the notion of overall degree of support, I turn in Section 3 to the notion of incremental confirmation of a hypothesis by evidence, sketching ways in which the Bayesian approach explains successes of the scientific method, improves on the qualitative accounts briefly mentioned in Section 1.5 and on other probability-based approaches, and ultimately provides a framework for induction. I respond there to some challenges to my proposal, while devoting the whole of Section 4 to what I see as the most significant obstacle facing any broadly Bayesian approach to evidential support, the problem of identifying and justifying an appropriate epistemic perspective to take on a given issue of theory choice. The online appendices take up some matters that do not fit given the tight constraints of this series, including some suggestions for further reading in Online Appendix A.

1 Induction and Inductive Logic

I begin in Section 1.1 with a discussion of induction characterised as a species of theoretical reasoning. A general account of theoretical reason goes well beyond the scope of this Element, but part of an account of inductive reasoning is understanding the reasons to which it responds, which in Section 1.2 I suggest are promisingly theorised as grounded in relations of evidential support. Section 1.3 distinguishes absolute evidential support from incremental evidential favouring, or confirmation; I will treat both in this Element. I briefly mention why this project might deserve to be called 'inductive logic' (Section 1.4).

In Section 1.5, I note one respect in which evidential support is unlike formal logic: whether some evidence supports a hypothesis doesn't depend on their content alone, but also on background knowledge. This dependence is so substantial that any adequate theory of evidential support must recognise it as a three-place relation between evidence, hypothesis, and background knowledge – background knowledge serving to fix how evidence bears on hypotheses. I argue in Section 1.6 that this observation was pre-empted by Hume in his discussion of induction in the *Enquiry*. Far from being fatal to the prospects of inductive logic, Hume's problem rather emphasises the need for a treatment that separates the structure of inductive reasons from their justification (Section 1.7).

1.1 Induction

Induction is a species of *inference*. It is distinguished from practical reason as it involves the reasoned adoption of new beliefs. It is distinguished from deduction in that the new beliefs are not logical consequences of the old. Induction is closely associated with scientific reasoning, what Hume called 'inferences from experience' (1999/1748, sec. 4.21): making predictions and reasoning from evidence to hypothesis.

Consider what happened when scientists adopted Hutton and Lyell's *Uniformitarian* approach to geology (Lyell 1830). Uniformitarians argued that the same geological processes (erosion, deposition, lithification, orogeny, etc.,) active today are also those responsible for shaping the landscape of the Earth throughout time. Ripple marks in an exposed vertical rock layer, far from the sea, demand an explanation. The Uniformitarian explains them as arising from the operation, over geological timescales, of familiar processes: postulating an ancient shallow sea in which the ripple marks were formed, the covering of those rippled layers by subsequent sediments, the gradual folding and uplift of the resulting sedimentary rock into a mountain range, and the erosion of that range over millions of years to reveal the ripples again to the eye (Drexel *et al.* 2012/1993, pp. 171–197).

In postulating this continuity between present and past geological processes, Uniformitarians endorse a canonical form of inductive inference. They reason from evidence of *observed* geological activity to predictions concerning the outcomes of *unobserved* geological activity. (Here, and throughout, evidence is treated as *propositional – that volcanic rocks intruded into older sedimentary rocks* is evidence, not the rocks themselves.) While most geological inference concerns what our evidence reveals about events of the distant past, Uniformitarianism also supports inference from past to future, perhaps a more traditional conception of inductive inference. This type of inference is at least parallel to *inverse inference* in statistics, reasoning from features of a known sample to those of the larger population from which it is drawn.

If accepted, Uniformitarianism would vindicate many inverse inferences. Its characteristic thesis is, in effect, the application to geology of what has come to be known as the *Uniformity Principle*:

> that instances, of which we have had no experience, must resemble those, of which we have had experience, and that the course of nature continues always uniformly the same. (Hume 2000/1739, sec. 1.3.6.4)

But what might justify the acceptance of Uniformitarianism itself? This appears to involve another scientific inference schema. Uniformitarians were opposed by *Catastrophists* (Gohau 1990 pp. 139–150), who proposed that various geological irregularities (discontinuities in the fossil record, unconformities in rock strata) were to be explained by currently unattested processes that dramatically transformed the earth over very short timescales. (Some were keen to link these ideas to flood narratives in various religious traditions.) Principal advantages of Uniformitarianism over Catastrophism include its simplicity and avoidance of ad hoc bespoke geological processes. Uniformitarianism is supported over Catastrophism, on the basis of the agreed geological evidence, by an *inference to the best explanation* (IBE) that takes these features to be truth-conducive virtues (Harman 1965; Henderson 2014; Lipton 2004). That is: the simpler and less ad hoc theory is regarded as better than its rivals, and indeed, good enough to meet a threshold for acceptance. The inference is motivated by the natural thought that a false theory would not be able to give such a simple and satisfactory account of the evidence. Darwin says as much in his description of this inference schema:

> It can hardly be supposed that a false theory would explain, in so satisfactory a manner as does the theory of natural selection, the several large classes of facts above specified. It has recently been objected that this is an unsafe method of arguing; but it is a method used in judging of the common events of life, and has often been used by the greatest natural philosophers. (Darwin 1876, p. 421)

As Darwin notes, IBE and inverse inference are both exemplified in ordinary reasoning as well as scientific contexts. We conclude that the last evening train will depart late, on the basis that it's always been late. We may also conclude in turn that something is a little different about the population of passengers who tend to take the last train, perhaps hypothesising that they are particularly prone to the sorts of behaviours that cause delays.

While there are interesting special features of inverse inference as opposed to the inference to the best explanation more generally, both exhibit an 'ampliative' character. In the example previously discussed, the Uniformitarian hypothesis is not a logical consequence of the given geological evidence, because Catastrophism is consistent with the evidence but incompatible with Uniformitarianism. Logical deduction may exclude hypotheses that are inconsistent with the evidence, but mere consistency does not favour one among the hypotheses consistent with the evidence. By contrast, reasonable inductive inference can lead us to favour one of many coherent hypotheses, as in the examples discussed previously. It is coherent to suppose the future quite unlike the past; yet we habitually infer that the future will broadly resemble the past. As such, inductive inference 'goes beyond' the evidence.

The central normative question about induction arises at this point. What, if anything, makes it reasonable to go beyond the evidence, by accepting one of many coherent hypotheses? Or, from the other end of the process, how was 'our hard-won factual knowledge . . . secured by any process of demonstrably sound reasoning' (Howson 2000, p. 1)? So stated, this is an enormously challenging question. It involves the identification, characterisation, and justification of inductive methods for forming beliefs in response to empirical evidence. A complete account of such methods will tackle many of the central issues in epistemology and philosophy of science, going well beyond the scope of this Element.

1.2 Inductive Reason and Evidential Support

My focus is narrower. Any inference is a 'reasoned change in view' (Harman 1986, p. 5). A theory of inference should then provide an account of the reasons involved, and what changes one should make to one's beliefs in light of them.

Consider deductive inference. The reasons in question are grounded in relations of implication: *that P logically implies $P \vee Q$*, for example. These provide reasons such as this: 'the fact that one's view logically implies P can be a reason to accept P' (Harman 1986, p. 11). This may be a reason, but it is hardly a decisive one; it depends what else one believes and the other reasons one has. So any account of deductive change in view should not entail that one must come to believe P when one's view logically implies P. Sometimes one should revise one's view to remove the implication; there are some formal theories of how to do that (Alchourrón *et al.* 1985).

It is rather tricky to state principles of belief revision that exceptionlessly cover all the possibly reasonable ways of responding to reasons provided by deductive logic (Harman 1986, chapter 2). Principles of reasoned change in view hold in general only *ceteris paribus*. Principles of belief revision involve balancing various reasons one has – one has a reason to avoid unmanageable clutter in one's beliefs, but also a reason to have opinions about the many and varied things one might encounter in one's environment, and these reasons may push in opposite directions. Finding the resultant force of various component epistemic reasons to rationalise a particular change in view is not an easy matter, and the reasons provided by logical implications do not trump other reasons. This makes inference quite unlike implication: while Q is implied by P of necessity if it is implied at all, Q may reasonably be inferred from P in some circumstances while not in others.

A general theory of theoretical reasoning, of how to respond to one's epistemic reasons, will include consideration of all the reasons one might have: those provided by deductive logic, testimony (Fricker 1995; Lackey 2008), memory (Fernández 2015; Lackey 2005), as well as empirical evidence and explanatory considerations of the sort considered in Section 1.1. There is nothing especially distinctively inductive about theoretical reason in general. But an appropriate topic for us, starting from an interest in scientific reasoning, is to focus on these 'inductive reasons' provided by evidence. This would involve principles about reasons that might parallel the defeasible reasons provided by logical implication. For example, IBE looks like it might be captured by something like this principle: *that P is the best explanation of some evidence you possess can be a reason to accept P* (Harman 1986, chapter 7). There will be parallel principles about the epistemic force of simplicity, strength, coherence, and so on.

The diversity of such principles may seem at first glance to be unmanageable. But in fact each may fall under a plausible general schema:

Evidential Support

That H is *supported by* the evidence can be a reason to accept H.

This schema concerns a general relation of evidential support. That relation also appears in other attractive principles governing theoretical reasoning, such as the claim that one ought to believe a hypothesis only if one's *total evidence* overall supports that hypothesis. Particular examples put substantive constraints on this notion. For example, the Uniformitarian thinks that current observations about geological processes support the claim that similar processes were operative in the distant past. This thought appears to involve a conception of evidential support that itself rests on Uniformitarian assumptions – namely, that nature is geologically uniform, broadly speaking. Those Uniformitarian assumptions are plausible (granting, e.g., the claim that evidence supports those hypotheses which best explain it – where 'best' here includes considerations of theoretical virtues such as simplicity, non-ad hoc-ness, explanatory strength, etc.). Yet it is worth noting that Catastrophists likely understand the evidential import and significance of current geological processes very differently.

1.3 Absolute and Incremental Support

The Evidential Support schema stands in need of clarification, as there are both *absolute* and *incremental* relations of evidential support, both of which can provide reasons to believe. (While our schema is ambiguous, it seems true on either disambiguation.) Absolute evidential support exists when a particular hypothesis is on balance overall most favoured by the total evidence. Incremental evidential support – what is often termed *confirmation* – exists when some evidence is in favour of a hypothesis. These notions come apart. Quite how they diverge will depend in part on the precise account of evidential support on offer (I'll follow this up in Section 3.1). But even before a precise model is on the table, there are intuitive cases where some evidence favours a hypothesis without absolutely supporting it; and there are cases where a hypothesis is on balance most supported while being disfavoured by some evidence:

- Many incompatible hypotheses can be supported by the evidence; at most one can be absolutely supported by the evidence. Suppose we are searching for a bushwalker, lost on a plateau. Lost walkers tend to follow drainage basins downstream (Koester 2008); we see there are four possible creeks they might have followed. Ground-based searchers have excluded one of them. This evidence favours (supports) all three remaining hypotheses about where the hiker might be without necessarily favouring any one in particular.
- If we have only a small sample, the evidence may favour a hypothesis without being sufficient to absolutely support it overall. A small survey yields evidence that all smokers in the sample have impaired lung capacity, and this evidence supports the hypothesis that all smokers have impaired lung capacity. However, the small sample size precludes that evidence being sufficient to warrant an inference to that conclusion.
- A positive result from a reliable medical diagnostic is evidence in favour of the hypothesis that one has the disease. But even reliable diagnostics are imperfect, giving rise to 'false positives' – cases where the test is positive but where the subject doesn't in fact have the disease. If a disease is rare in the population, a good diagnostic test can favour the hypothesis that one has the illness without making it overall credible – it may just be rendered more credible than it would have been in the absence of that evidence. (This is an example of the relevance of the 'base rate'; see Section 3.3.)

- This is a good example of the way that a hypothesis can be supported overall while being disconfirmed. A positive test result makes it slightly less incredible that one has a rare disease, but not sufficiently so to make that hypothesis acceptable.

Both absolute and incremental supports provide epistemic reasons. Neither suffices to determine the outcome of inductive reasoning: even if H is overall most credible in light of evidence, there may be reasons to suspend judgement, or to change one's mind about other things. A belief in H needn't result from the acquisition of evidence that overall supports H.

The project that now comes into view is to offer a general characterisation of absolute and incremental evidential support, as relations that may obtain between any hypothesis and any body of evidence such that had it 'actually obtained, [it] would constitute favourable evidence for' that hypothesis (Hempel 1945a, p. 2). (Notice Hempel's formulation exhibits the same ambiguity in 'evidence for'.) When applied in scientific practice, perhaps the vital questions concern which among the hypotheses that are presently live for us are supported by the actual evidence. But the theory of evidential support is more general.

1.4 Inductive Logic

Deductive logic is the study of consequence relations. Those consequence relations underlie the coherence and completeness of various states of belief, and those features yield some special cases of evidential support, for example, that if the evidence logically entails P, then P is supported by the evidence, or if Q is inconsistent with the evidence, then Q is not supported by the evidence. So the relation of evidential support should have deductive consequence as a special case. This is captured in this widely accepted condition:

Entailment Condition
If some evidence E entails a distinct non-trivial hypothesis H, then E (absolutely and incrementally) supports H. (cf. Hempel 1945b, p. 103)

If the study of deductive consequence is deductive logic, the study of these more general notions of evidential support might well be termed *inductive logic*. The suggestion is that this would be an apt label for the attempt to offer quite general and abstract structural features of evidential support relations, in roughly the way that deductive logic captures quite general and abstract structural features of conclusive evidential support. This is the project I will explore in this Element, pursuing what Strevens (2004) calls an 'inductive framework'.

There is no guarantee that factoring an account of theoretical inductive reasoning into a story about inductive reasons (which I am identifying with the theory of evidential support) and a story about changes in view (an account of the dynamics of belief) will bear fruit. Perhaps the right way to think about the matter involves no such division; or perhaps the right way to think about inductive reasons is not in terms of incremental evidential support. The only way to proceed here is to attempt to construct a theory of evidential support, and evaluate the project of inductive logic in light of the fruits or failures of that attempt. That, in any case, is the constructive spirit behind my approach.

1.5 Formality and Background Knowledge

Early proponents of inductive logic pursued the project in an ambitious and literal fashion, attempting to pin down, using formal resources alone, a notion of support of a conclusion by some premises that would generalise the notion of logical consequence. Conclusiveness is all-or-nothing, but inconclusive evidence supports hypotheses to varying degrees, so any such inductive logic must say something about which invalid argument forms are nevertheless 'logically confirming' in virtue of the logical properties of their constituents. Let us for now introduce the (non-standard) symbol ' $\Vdash$ ' to denote this (still hypothetical) relation of logical confirmation; $\Gamma \Vdash \phi$ says that the premises Γ logically confirm ϕ.

Any premises should logically confirm any of their logical consequences: if $\Gamma \vDash \phi$ then $\Gamma \Vdash \phi$. But that is where the similarity to classical deductive logic ceases. For one thing, even if $\Gamma \Vdash \phi$, it need not be that $\Gamma, \psi \Vdash \phi$. Some premises about balls drawn from an opaque bag known to contain 100 balls might be 'ball 1 is red', 'ball 2 is red', ..., 'ball 99 is red'. Suppose these premises logically confirm the conclusion that all the balls in the bag are red. But add the premise 'ball 100 is black' to the others, and that conclusion is definitely not supported. This feature of a consequence relation is known as *non-monotonicity* (Hawthorne 2021, section 2.2; Straßer forthcoming). Another disanalogy is that while logical consequence is *transitive* (if $\phi \vDash \psi$ and $\psi \vDash \chi$, then $\phi \vDash \chi$), logical confirmation is not. Shogenji (2003, p. 613) gives the following example: that X is an academic philosopher confirms that X has a PhD; that X has a PhD confirms that X is well-paid; but it does not follow that X's being an academic philosopher confirms that X is well-paid.

These features are logically unusual, but arguably must be captured by any adequate inductive logic. They are already suggestive of the thought that logical features of sentences are not going to match up with what we want from an inductive logic. This suggestion is correct. Consider this principle, which is about the most plausible example of purely logical confirmation: that instances confirm generalisations:

Nicod's Condition

A universal generalisation *that all Fs are Gs* is supported by any instance of *an F which is a G*. (Hempel 1945a, p. 10)

In my notation, $(Fa \wedge Ga) \Vdash \forall x(Fx \rightarrow Gx)$.

Famously, Nicod's Condition appears subject to counterexample. Direct counterexamples have been offered (Good 1961; Howson & Urbach 1993, p. 129; Swinburne 1971, p. 326), and the principle is one of the main drivers of Hempel's famous 'paradox of the ravens' (Section 3.5). Unfortunately, without Nicod's Condition, Hempel's remaining purely formal principles are far too weak to pin down any definite notion of evidential support (Earman 1992, p. 66ff). Other proposed additional principles, such as the Converse Consequence Condition (Hempel 1945b, p. 104; Moretti 2003), are subject to not-unrelated counterexamples. It appears that a theory of evidential support must draw on resources more substantive than those provided by formal logic. (However, something of a revival of a syntactic approach to confirmation may be found in Carnap's work – see Section 4.4.)

Counterexamples to Nicod's Condition offer a general lesson. Sometimes, an instance supports a generalisation; sometimes, a generalisation is undermined by an instance. Consider a slight modification of one of Good's cases:

> Suppose that we know we are in one or other of two worlds, and the hypothesis, *H*, under consideration is that all the crows in our world are black. We know in advance that in one world there are a hundred black crows, no crows that are not black, and a million other birds; and that in the other world there are a thousand black crows, one white one, and a [hundred] other birds. A bird is selected equiprobably at random from all the birds in our world. It turns out to be a black crow. This is strong evidence . . . that we are in the second world, wherein not all crows are black. Thus the observation of a black crow, in the circumstances described, undermines the hypothesis that all the crows in our world are black. (Good 1967, p. 322)

This case shows that the evidence – seeing a black crow – is variably supportive of the hypothesis that all crows are black, depending on the background conditions – in this case, background knowledge of the space of possibilities. Seeing a black crow under the circumstances described is only unsurprising in the second world, and is thus strong evidence that we occupy the second world; thus an instance turns out to be strong evidence *against* the generalisation that all crows are black. But under our typical assumptions about the background space of possibilities, that same evidence is evidence *for* the generalisation. Evidential support is not a relation between hypothesis and evidence alone, and a fortiori is not an internal relation (one necessitated by its relata). Support is in that respect disanalogous to logical entailment.

Evidential support is not merely formal in character (Hawthorne 2021, section 2.3), even when we can say quite general things about the form of any relation of evidential support (see Section 2.4). But a framework for evidential support stops short of giving any concrete indication of which evidence supports which claims. Successful induction is grounded not just in the formal structure of the evidence, but in its content. As Norton says 'particular facts in each domain license the inductive inferences admissible in that domain' (Norton 2003, p. 648). The most straightforward way to capture this observation (admittedly, not Norton's own) is to explicitly relativise and represent confirmation as 'a three-place relation ("E confirms H relative to K") [since] background knowledge can make a crucial difference to confirmation' (Earman 1992, p. 67).

This suggestion immediately allows us to represent the way that statistical inference depends on a background probability model (Fitelson 2006, section 4). Suppose we are drawing from an urn of known constitution, containing two red and two black balls. Against a background probability model involving drawing with replacement, the evidence that the first two draws were both red provides no support for the hypothesis that the next draw will be red: the trials do not influence one another and each is accurately represented by the same probability model (they are *independent and identically distributed*, or 'IID'). But in the context of a background model involving drawing *without* replacement, that same evidence is conclusive support for the hypothesis that the next draw is black.

The background information is not just more evidence; we cannot collapse evidential support back to a two-place relation. In the previous example, that the draws are independent is not a piece of evidence alongside the fact that the first draw was red. The assumption of independence provides a framework into which both evidence and hypothesis must fit, to allow it to constrain how a given body of evidence bears on hypotheses.

1.6 Hume's Problem

In the foregoing example, the adoption of a particular stochastic model is itself likely the upshot of some inductive reasoning. That the trials are IID is a hypothesis justified on the basis of evidence (perhaps evidence about outcome frequencies or about the mechanisms involved in drawing from and mixing up the urn). The evidence itself only yields inductive reasons in the context of some inductive framework.

Hume's infamous 'problem of induction' can be seen to rest on an early recognition of this point (Henderson 2022). Hume recognised that our inductive habits rested on the pattern of causal relationships evident in our experience, and the 'supposition' that future patterns 'will be conformable to the past' (Hume 1999/1748, para. 4.19):

> all inferences from experience suppose, as their foundation, that the future will resemble the past, and that similar powers will be conjoined with similar sensible qualities. If there be any suspicion, that the course of nature may change, and that the past may be no rule for the future, all experience becomes useless, and can give rise to no inference or conclusion. It is impossible, therefore, that any arguments from experience can prove this resemblance of the past to the future; since all these arguments are founded on the supposition of that resemblance. Let the course of things be allowed hitherto ever so regular; that alone, without some new argument or inference, proves not, that, for the future, it will continue so. (Hume 1999/1748, para. 4.21)

Hume frames the question as one about the reasons evidence about the past provides for beliefs about the future course of nature. He doesn't explicitly invoke evidential support. But his target, that the past provides a 'rule for the future', is fairly clearly a claim about evidential support for hypotheses about the future by evidence about the past. His aim, in my terminology, is to reveal what reasons there are for us to adopt an inductive framework $\mathcal{F}$ in which the past provides a rule for the future. His worry is one of circularity: that any reasons to adopt framework $\mathcal{F}$ are themselves only reasons on the presupposition of $\mathcal{F}$. For those are reasons drawn from our evidence about the past, and our views about how that evidence bears on hypotheses are likewise grounded in how past evidence bore on past hypotheses. When Hume emphasises the possibility 'that the course of nature may change', he is not merely pointing out a difference between induction and deduction. He is pointing out that our grasp on relations of evidential support is itself dependent on our evidential history. More concisely: any general hypotheses about the nature and structure of evidential support we adopt can only be for reasons that presuppose those same hypotheses about evidential support (Howson 2000, pp. 10–15).

1.7 The Justification of Induction and the Structure of Evidential Support

Hume's resolution of his problem is characteristically bold. He claims that our inductive inferences are but 'a species of natural instincts, which no reasoning or process of the thought and understanding is able, either to produce, or to prevent' (Hume 1999/1748, para. 5.8). As I would approach the question, Hume here acknowledges the dependence of evidential support on a background inductive framework, and suggests that our adoption of such a framework is not itself the product of reasons and hence need not wait on a further prior inductive framework.

What does Hume's naturalistic explanation of our inductive habits tell us about evidential support? In one way, it merely underscores the result from Section 1.5 that evidential support must be understood as a three-place relation between evidence, hypotheses, and an explicit relativisation to some background inductive framework or assumptions. The fact that the same evidence can bear differently on hypotheses in different worldly circumstances, while those worldly circumstances may not themselves be known to us, suggests that it may not generally be possible to justify the adoption of any such framework.

We don't need to follow Hume in his scepticism about inductive frameworks. It might well be that we can, ultimately, find a justification for accepting a particular conception of evidential support. For example, perhaps some conception of how evidence bears on hypotheses is justified by default, or we might have justification for some inductive assumptions 'without being in a position to cite anything that could count as ampliative, non-question-begging evidence for those beliefs' (Pryor 2000, p. 520). Perhaps we acquire our inductive habits of thought by testimony, deference, or immersion in a scientific community, and justification comes subsequent to the fruits of our epistemic endeavours. Perhaps we are justified simply because 'the world is so constituted that inductive arguments lead on the whole to true opinions' (Ramsey 1990, p. 93). These would all be ways in which an inductive framework could be adopted without internalistic justification of the sort Hume appears to seek.

However such justification might be acquired, it is fruitful to separate the question of how to *justify* a particular view about the bearing of evidence on hypotheses from the question of the *structure* of evidential support. The latter issue can be pursued to a significant extent by characterising the three-way connections between evidence, hypotheses, and standards of evidential support, without taking a stand on what the actual evidence is, what the actually live hypotheses are, or what the actual standards of evidential support are. Because this investigation concerns the abstract structural features of this three-place relation 'E supports H relative to inductive framework F', it is a deserving bearer of the label 'inductive logic'. (Though to illustrate its significance, it will be helpful to give at least some examples of how the relata can be concretely filled in.)

That is how I will pursue inductive logic in this Element. In particular, I will explore *Bayesianism*, a particularly influential and fruitful approach to the formal features of evidential support. Bayesians propose that an inductive framework can be represented by a probability function, which captures both any relevant background information and encodes (in its conditional probabilities) a conception of absolute evidential relevance. A Bayesian conception of inductive frameworks is presented in Section 2, where roughly the following account is offered: the evidence absolutely supports H, relative to some probability model, just when H is more probable than not, conditional on E. That same model also allows us to represent a comparative notion of confirmation: to regard E as confirming H is to regard H as more probable given E than otherwise. The Bayesian theory of confirmation and its consequences is the subject of Section 3. I will return to the issue Hume raises, of how to justify inductive assumptions, in Section 3.7. We delve further into whether there are significant prior constraints on what sorts of probability models we may permissibly adopt in Section 4, including some consideration of Goodman's (1954) 'new riddle' of induction (Section 4.4).

2 Probability and Evidential Support

In this section, I discuss how probability theory can be used to understand the notion of an inductive framework. We consider one useful motivating metaphor, that of the *prospects* of truth and falsity of a given proposition. The idea of a prospect builds in relativity to a perspective, that is, what comes into view from the vantage of a given body of evidence. Epistemic perspectives are described in Section 2.1, and their connection with the rationalisation of idealised bets is made clear in Section 2.2. Constraints on the proper evaluation of bets then constrain legitimate measures of prospects (Section 2.3). Indeed, the constraints ensure that every legitimate measure of prospects is an *evidential probability function* (Section 2.4), so I spend some time characterising the principles governing these probability functions, and introducing in a brief manner the mathematics of probability. The argument from Section 2.3 is a version of a *Dutch Book Argument*, and I delve into the differences between my version and more standard versions in Section 2.5. In Section 2.6, I turn to conditional probability, the prospects of hypotheses given other claims, which will be central to the account of absolute evidential support and incremental confirmation (recall Section 1.3). Finally, in Section 2.8, I turn to the epistemic question of how to choose or rationalise a choice of epistemic perspective, and touch on the topics of epistemic deference and the debate over permissivism in epistemology.

2.1 Prospects and Perspectives

The *prospects* for a hypothesis are – not wholly metaphorically – what is in view in light of some body of evidence. (Note the related but distinct usage by Kahneman & Tversky (1979).) A hypothesis which is supported by some potential evidence has an *improved* prospect of turning out to be true when that potential evidence is gathered. What is visually in prospect for you depends on where you are *and* on the direction you are facing: your perspective. Likewise, what is *epistemically* in prospect depends on your epistemic perspective: where you find yourself evidentially as well as on the significance of that position in the space of possibilities.

Camp characterises occupying an epistemic perspective as having 'an open-ended disposition to characterise: to encounter, interpret, and respond to some parts of the world in certain ways' (2019, p. 24). That is what it is to *occupy* a perspective. A perspective itself need not be embodied, existing independently of any agent occupying it, but it must suffice to characterise such dispositions. To fulfil that role, I suggest that each epistemic perspective must involve the following:

1. A representation of a space of possibilities;
2. A representation of the total evidence currently on hand; and
3. Some policy, or set of standards (Schoenfield 2012, p. 199), that capture, numerically, the significance of potential evidence for various entertainable hypotheses.

Let me expand on these components. 'A space of possibilities' captures all the ways that things might have turned out and might yet turn out, at least according to that perspective. It is natural to take this space of possibilities to have the structure of a *field* of propositions (Eagle 2011, pp. 1–3; Hájek & Hitchcock 2017, p. 17). That is, for each outcome that might occur, according to that perspective, there is a proposition in the field to the effect that the outcome comes to pass; there is a trivial outcome, represented by a trivially true proposition (i.e., that something or other comes to pass); and whenever the field of propositions includes P and Q, it also includes $\neg P$, $(P \vee Q)$, and $(P \wedge Q)$. A maximally specific possibility will be represented by a logically complex proposition that fixes, for each possible outcome, whether or not it occurs. This will play the role of a 'possible world' from that perspective. I will often work with collections of propositions $\{P_1, \ldots, P_n\}$ such that no two of them are true in a single possible world, and at least one is true in every possible world. Such a collection is called a *partition*. The set of all possible worlds is a partition, but so are various more coarse-grained divisions of the space of apparent possibilities, for example, a complete set of possible experimental outcomes.

I will not distinguish propositions true of exactly the same possibilities; depending on how possibilities themselves are individuated, this may or may not mean identifying with one another those propositions that have, necessarily, the same truth value (Stalnaker 1984, p. 2). These possibilities thus need not be 'metaphysically possible', nor must each metaphysical possibility be among those represented in a perspective – they are potential epistemic (or perhaps doxastic) possibilities (Titelbaum 2022, pp. 27–38).

It must be acknowledged that different perspectives needn't agree on how to analyse any given proposition into more specific outcomes. There is no guarantee that all perspectives will agree on what the most fine-grained possibilities are, or on which propositions are possible. I will assume that there are perspectives capable of representing any hypotheses or pieces of evidence we might need to consider. Even so, some perspectives – something like those Savage called 'small worlds' (Savage 1954, p. 16) – might be very limited, able to represent only a narrow range of hypotheses and evidence. (We might consider the possible outcomes of an experiment, and the hypotheses on which they bear, without including any possibilities in which the experiment was never performed at all.) The question of what happens when an agent manages to expand their conception of what is possible is philosophically very rich and much discussed – sometimes under the label of 'partition sensitivity' – but lies beyond the scope of this Element (Paul 2014; Pettigrew 2020a).

An epistemic perspective must also represent a body of total evidence. Evidence constrains which possibilities in the space of possibilities are left open and which are excluded. Because evidence is propositional, evidence narrows down a location in the space of possibilities by excluding those possibilities in which propositions inconsistent with the evidence are true (Stalnaker 1984, p. 120). So an epistemic perspective can represent the current total evidence by indicating in some way a region of the space of possibilities which, from that perspective, might be actual – those consistent with the evidence.

Finally, and most importantly for inductive logic, an epistemic perspective must represent in some way the bearing of the evidence on the remaining live hypotheses. It must provide a way of discriminating among all those hypotheses not ruled out by the evidence. I will assume that this discrimination is effected numerically; so an epistemic perspective assigns numbers to hypotheses that somehow reflect their support by the evidence. As Horwich puts it, 'our inductive practice may be represented by a function which specifies, for any evidential circumstance, the permissible degrees of belief in any statement' (1982, p. 79). Such a function will be an epistemic perspective, noting that it is not to be identified with one's actual attitudes (one's 'degrees of belief', in Horwich's treatment), but circumscribes permissible attitudes.

An epistemic perspective thus represents a possible way of 'proportion[ing] belief to the evidence' (Hume 1999/1748, sec. 10.4). A proportioning will in general assign different numbers to hypotheses, even those it regards as on balance supported by the evidence. That evidential support varies in extent is fairly commonsensical. Suppose that my current total evidence supports the claim that it is raining outside my office right now, and that it also supports the claim that the weather next weekend will be very hot. It would be foolish to deny that it may support the former to a considerably greater extent than it supports the latter. That this variability in evidential support can be quantified numerically is a reasonable starting point.[1]

Someone's actual attitudes may not correspond to any epistemic perspective. For example, they may have incoherent or indeterminate attitudes to a hypothesis, precluding the assignment of a single number as the degree to which the evidence supports it. Perhaps at best an imprecise range of attitudes could be ascribed to them (Jeffrey 1983a, pp. 139–140). And an epistemic perspective need not correspond to anyone's actual state of belief or knowledge. But an epistemic perspective does appear to be something a rational agent could have as an ideal for a coherent body of epistemic attitudes. To put it in explicitly normative terms, an epistemic perspective has a structure that any reasonable total system of epistemic attitudes must approximate, and provides a regulative ideal for such attitudes (see Section 2.8). (If there are reasonable yet indeterminate systems of epistemic attitudes, then perhaps the regulative norm should be that any such state can be precisified into one or more determinate epistemic perspectives.) Epistemic perspectives rationalise the states of belief and knowledge of any agents who occupy them.

Given this, one way of describing the present project is that we begin from the assumption that all epistemic perspectives are rational, and use that fact to establish the properties that distinguish epistemic perspectives from other purported evaluations of the prospects of hypotheses.

2.2 Prospects and Bets

If an epistemic perspective represents the prospects of hypotheses, it must be subject to certain norms about the evaluation of prospects. One way to bring out these norms is to consider the ideal evaluation of *bets* (de Finetti 1964/1937; Pettigrew 2020b; Ramsey 1990). This is not because one is likely to be involved in 'betting on theories' (Maher 1993). Rather, among the dispositions involved in adopting a perspective are dispositions to evaluate, as favourable or otherwise, wagers on hypotheses about how things are, given an exogenously settled assignment of values to outcomes. If there are constraints on the acceptability of

---

[1] Reasonable, but not obligatory: we could begin instead with comparative claims (Konek 2019; Koopman 1940; Neth 2025; Stefánsson 2017).

evaluations, those constraints may reveal structural features of epistemic perspectives that rationalise those evaluations.

At first glance, it might seem that we should assign prospects to hypotheses by trying to elicit betting behaviour and infer an epistemic perspective from it. Witness Kyburg's insistence that 'how seriously someone believes what he says he believes' is elicited by inviting him 'to put his money where his mouth is' (1983, p. 64). This is unlikely to succeed, given the confounding factors in real-life gambling behaviour, which is psychologically and logistically complicated, not to say morally fraught. The declining marginal utility of money (Pettigrew 2020b, pp. 17–19), the difficulty of finding parties and counterparties to every possible bet, the fact that some outcomes will be resolved only after the agent's lifespan if ever, the fact of risk-averse and risk-seeking individuals (Buchak 2013; Kahneman & Tversky 1979), all make it difficult to draw direct conclusions about the prospects of P from an agent's (un)willingness to bet on P. It is complicated to deduce an agent's own mental state from the betting prices they offer (Bradley & Leitgeb 2006), let alone an epistemic perspective legitimising their attitudes.

Nevertheless, behind any reasoned decision to bet lies an epistemic perspective: some evaluation of the prospects of the propositions one is betting on, given the evidence one has (Howson & Urbach 1993, pp. 76–77). That the prospects of a proposition are decent can go some way towards *justifying* taking a bet, without constituting, or being constituted by, anyone's actual willingness to bet. Doubtless that epistemic perspective justifies other dispositions too – perhaps dispositions to assert, or to employ hypotheses in scientific explanation. But betting has a neat connection to evaluation which makes these dispositions of particular interest for us here, despite the suspicion that assertion and explanation are of greater importance.

A *bet* on a proposition H is a right to receive s units of value if H turns out to be true, and nothing otherwise. The price of the bet is the value x that is assigned to that right. (So we can imagine a bet on a coin toss as a right to receive \$10 if the coin lands tails, and a bookmaker could decide to price this right at \$7.) For each bet, there is a *counterbet*, which is a bet against H that yields s units if H turns out to be false and which costs $s - x$ units. The payout s is the total staked, the sum of the units of value contributed jointly by the bet and counterbet, $s = x + (s - x)$. (In the example, the bookmaker is implicitly taking the counterbet, putting up \$3 for the right to receive \$10 if the coin does not land tails.) For simplicity, let us restrict attention to bets where the total stake s is 1 unit. We can treat a counterbet against H at $s - x$ as equivalent to a bet on $\neg H$ at that same price. This is justified by this basic principle of *equivalence*: any bets which have the same payoffs in the same circumstances must rationally be assigned the same price. A bet against H that costs $s - x$ to yield s pays off when H is false; as does a bet on $\neg H$ with the same cost and yield.[2]

Real agents only enter into bets they regard as favourable. (We have not assumed that stakes are monetary; an agent who loves the thrill of gambling may find a bet favourable while it is unfavourable in purely monetary terms.) A bet on H is favourable, intuitively, if the prospect of gaining the payout s more than compensates for the risk of losing what you have staked x. We have assumed that an epistemic perspective represents prospects numerically. Suppose that relative to a given perspective the prospect of H is p. A bet is favourable if the payout, weighted by the prospect of getting the payout, exceeds the cost: $ps > x$. A bet is unfavourable if $ps < x$; a case where the prospect of gain is outweighed by the risk of loss. An agent is epistemically justified in entering into a bet only if the bet is favourable-from-their-perspective. (This is a necessary condition for all-things-considered justification for a bet, but is not sufficient.)

What if the prospect of gain and the risk of loss are exactly balanced according to some perspective? Such a bet is *neutrally* priced. The potential bettor lacks positive reason to enter into a neutrally priced bet; the prospect of gain is too little. But nor is the bet unfavourable; the prospect of loss isn't sufficiently great to motivate a favourable evaluation of the counterbet. It would not be reasonable to prefer to accept a neutrally-priced bet or its counterbet over the status quo, given the prospects involved. *Thus a neutrally-priced bet will represent an accurate evaluation of the prospects of H according to an epistemic perspective*: it is a bet on H that is calibrated to the degree to which the evidence supports H. I will say that the numerical prospect of H, revealed in a neutrally priced bet on H from a particular perspective, is the *degree of support* that perspective provides to H.

2.3 Evaluating Prospects

To assign a neutral price to a bet would involve fixing on some particular epistemic perspective. The general structural principles on epistemic perspectives we are concerned with can be uncovered without making assumptions about neutral prices except that they exist. We uncover those general structural constraints – constraints that, it will turn out, suffice to ensure neutral prices are mathematically like probabilities (Section 2.4) – by noting that unless certain constraints are placed on the numerical evaluation of prospects, certain bets (and packages of bets) seem to yield an incoherent evaluation of their value.

---

[2] This assumes that the logic of negation, and structure of the space of propositions, is classical; constructing probabilistic epistemic perspectives given a non-classical logic involves several diverting challenges (Williams 2016).

Presented one way, the bets have a certain neutral price; presented another way, they are assigned another non-neutral price. So a single neutral price doesn't exist unless we constrain the acceptable numerical representation of evidential support in some way.

In particular, suppose an epistemic perspective could assign a prospect $-\delta$ to a proposition H, where $\delta > 0$. Such a perspective entails that the neutral price for a bet *on H* that pays 1 unit is $-\delta$. But at that price, there is an advantage to purchasing the bet – the price is negative, so, win or lose, represents an advantage over the status quo. A perspective that assigns a negative number as the degree to which the evidence supports H leads to a situation where the agent cannot assign a coherent neutral price. Their assessment of the prospects of H leads them to be indifferent to accepting this bet, while an assessment of the possible payoff of the bet should make them positively disposed to accept it. So this epistemic perspective turns out to be unable to assign a single value to the bet. To assign a neutral price to a bet, no perspective could assign a degree of support less than zero. That is, every epistemic perspective must satisfy:

Non-negativity

The degree of support provided by any body of evidence for a hypothesis H must be greater than or equal to zero.

This argument could be resisted if the neutral price of a bet depends on how the bet is described. If bets are individuated very finely, it might be that there is an advantage over the status quo when the bet is described one way, and not another. But it is not easy to see how this would work. The advantage or disadvantage of a bet is due to the conditional rights to valuable goods they convey. If one bet conveys at least as much as another, no matter what, one cannot rationally prefer the second to the first, regardless how it is described. To do so would be 'absurd', as Ramsey says: any account of prospects

> which broke [this principle] would be inconsistent in the sense that it violated the laws of preference between options, such as that preferability is a transitive asymmetrical relation, and that if α is preferable to β, β for certain cannot be preferable to α if p, β if not-p. (Ramsey 1990, p. 78; Skyrms 1987, pp. 227–228)

Since in this case $1 + \delta$ is preferable to δ, the bet on H that costs $-\delta$ is preferable to δ for sure; and δ for sure is preferable to the status quo, transitivity of preference ensures that the bet cannot be neutrally priced at $-\delta$.

As this case shows, an epistemic perspective violating Non-negativity justifies inconsistent evaluations of the very same option. That inconsistency is what excludes it from being a genuine perspective on the prospects of H; the betting setup is simply a way to make this inconsistency manifest. The same sort of argument can be given for other constraints on epistemic perspectives.

Suppose that an epistemic perspective assigned a degree of support $\delta < 1$ to a trivial hypothesis H – one that was necessary, according to that perspective (obtaining in every possibility considered by that perspective). Such an epistemic perspective would regard as neutrally priced a bet on H priced at δ. Such a bet is certain to pay off; for such a perspective regards H as already true. So this bet cannot be neutrally priced at δ; for there is a guaranteed advantage to purchasing it, hence it is not to be regarded with indifference from the status quo. So for the same reasons as previously discussed, no epistemic perspective could assign a degree of support to a certain outcome that was less than 1:

Normality
The degree of support provided by any body of evidence for a trivial hypothesis (necessary in light of that evidence) is 1.

Finally, suppose that there are two hypotheses, H and H', such that the truth of either one excludes the truth of the other, according to some epistemic perspective. Suppose an epistemic perspective assigns a degree of support α to H, and degree of support β to H', and a degree of support δ to their disjunction $H \vee H'$, but where $\delta \neq \alpha + \beta$. The neutral prices for bets on these propositions H, H', and $H \vee H'$ are fixed by those degrees of support. Consider the book of bets consisting of bets on H and H' that each pay 1 unit; its payoffs are depicted in Table 1.

It is easy to see from the table that where $H \vee H'$ is true (the top two possibilities), the payoff is $1 - (\alpha + \beta)$, and when $H \vee H'$ is false, the payoff is $-(\alpha + \beta)$. But the neutral price for a bet on $H \vee H'$ is δ, leading to a different payoff of $1 - \delta$ when true, and $-\delta$ when false. So the book of bets pays out the same amount, in the same circumstances, as the individual bet on the disjunction – but has a different neutral price. Clearly, this either violates the equivalence requirement to assign the same neutral price to bets that pay off in the same circumstances, or violates the requirement on epistemic perspectives that we assign a single neutral price to a given bet. Hence:

Table 1 Payoffs for the book of bets on H and H'.

H	H'	**Bet on H**	**Bet on H'**	**Total payoff**	$H \vee H'$
T	F	$1 - \alpha$	$-\beta$	$1 - (\alpha + \beta)$	T
F	T	$-\alpha$	$1 - \beta$	$1 - (\alpha + \beta)$	T
F	F	$-\alpha$	$-\beta$	$-(\alpha + \beta)$	F

Additivity

The degree of support provided by any body of evidence for a disjunction of mutually exclusive hypotheses is the sum of the degrees of support provided to each hypothesis individually.

One further principle is implicated in establishing Additivity as a requirement on epistemic perspectives: the *package principle* that the neutral price for the book is the sum of the neutral prices for the bets, that is, 'that the value I set on them together is the sum of the values I set on them singly' (Earman 1992, p. 42; Schick 1986, p. 113; Titelbaum 2022, pp. 326–329). This package principle is plausible when one evaluates a package of bets offered all at once, especially given that we are considering the price that is justified, not the price that someone's wallet can withstand. (Add sufficiently many advantageously priced bets together and there will come an advantageously priced bet that one would purchase offered alone, but cannot afford.) The principle is less obvious when bets are offered sequentially rather than simultaneously (Schick 1986, pp. 116–118).

2.4 Probabilities and Degrees of Support

The argument of the previous section reached the conclusion that epistemic perspectives must satisfy Non-negativity, Normality, and Additivity to assign a single neutral price for a bet on each proposition in their scope. A numerical function from propositions which satisfies these constraints is, mathematically speaking, a *probability function* (Eagle 2011, pp. 1–4; Hájek & Hitchcock 2017; Kolmogorov 1956/1933). So it turns out that an epistemic perspective assigns probabilistic prospects to every proposition in its field (Section 2.1).

Satisfying these constraints is also sufficient for justifying a single neutral price (Kemeny 1955; Lehman 1955). Epistemic perspectives can accordingly be represented as *evidential probability* functions, assigning numbers to hypotheses, representing degrees of support, in light of the total evidence to which a perspective is committed. In line with Section 2.1, the total evidence according to an evidential probability function comprises those propositions which are assigned probability 1. This usage might be slightly revisionary, liberalising our conception of evidence so that it includes at a given moment any proposition on which we rely in evaluating other claims with which we are confronted. 'Taking the evidence into consideration' doesn't mean only taking things you happen to have learned empirically into consideration.

The argument in Section 2.3 showed that epistemic perspectives have the formal features common to all probability functions. Some have suggested that epistemic perspectives might obey tighter constraints. (I discuss these proposed constraints in the Online Appendix B.) For example, some have suggested that the evidential probabilities representing them should be *regular* (assigning zero probability only to impossibilities, or perhaps only to contradictions). More have suggested that evidential probabilities should obey a stronger Additivity constraint, *countable Additivity*. I do not insist that these are features of every epistemic perspective, though they may be features of some.

This approach to evidential probability has precedent in the literature. As argued in Section 2.1, epistemic perspectives rationalise the dispositions of their occupants to judge hypotheses. Thus we agree in part with Williamson (2000), who suggests that evidential probability represents the degree to which 'the evidence tells for or against the hypothesis' (2000, p. 209), rather than reflecting anyone's actual credences. Williamson's own view is that evidential probability should reflect 'something like the intrinsic plausibility of hypotheses prior to investigation' (2000, p. 211). On the present view, this only captures some epistemic perspectives, omitting those one can come to occupy *after* some investigation. Climenhaga puts it well: 'the distinctive claims of the degree-of-support interpretation [of evidential probability] are that probabilities are mind-independent relations between propositions and that probabilities constrain rational degrees of belief' (Climenhaga 2024, p. 3).

The tradition of *objective Bayesianism* that Climenhaga and Williamson represent goes back at least to Keynes (1921), Johnson (1932), and Carnap (1962). It has however almost invariably been accompanied with an additional and not necessarily welcome commitment to there being such a thing as '*the* degree to which evidence supports a hypothesis'. While each epistemic perspective on my view articulates a conception of how evidence bears on hypotheses, there is no commitment to the existence of a 'best' perspective. Perspectives – for all I've established so far – might disagree with one another on the space of possibilities, on the background evidence they incorporate, or on the significance they attach to it. We return to the question of whether there is a unique best perspective in Sections 2.8 and 4. For now, I would wish to distance the view defended here both from the 'subjective' Bayesian, who identifies epistemic perspectives with the actual degrees of belief of individual agents, and from the objective Bayesian who accepts a unique best perspective. The view I'm defending could be called *non-subjective Bayesianism*.

2.5 Probabilities and the Dutch Book Argument

In Section 2.3, I presented a version of what is known as the Dutch Book Argument (DBA) for the conclusion that degrees of support must be probabilities

(Eagle 2011, pp. 28–32; Hájek 2008; Howson & Urbach 1993, pp. 75–81; Pettigrew 2020b). The earliest versions of this argument were due to Ramsey (1990) and de Finetti (1964/1937); many variants have been offered since.

The typical DBA looks rather different from the version I have presented, however. The typical version applies to credences (degrees of belief), not to epistemic perspectives (degrees of support). A more important difference is the following. I argued that non-probabilistic assignments of numbers to hypotheses fail to reflect the prospects of those hypotheses (see also Armendt 1992, p. 218; Christensen 2004, p. 121; Titelbaum 2022, section 9.2.1). By contrast, the standard DBA argues that non-probabilistic credences are *practically* unreasonable because they subject those who act on such credences to a sure loss: 'Dutch Book arguments evaluate the rationality of credences by looking at the quality of the choices that they do or should lead us to make' (Pettigrew 2020b, p. 1). There is some connection with choices in the argument in Section 2.3, because an epistemic perspective is supposed to justify a neutral price for a bet, which may partly rationalise choices to bet at non-neutral prices. But the standard DBA relies on a much stronger link with choice, namely, that non-probabilistic credences rationally require the agent to commit to a package of bets that guarantees a sure loss.

These features of the DBA I've offered may help defuse some challenges that face more standard versions. The standard version is accused of being unrealistic (because real agents don't have sufficiently many determinate betting preferences for the argument to succeed), or because probabilism is descriptively inaccurate of real agents (Kyburg 1978). Defenders of the standard DBA have tried to fend off the accusation that it requires us to postulate a plethora of bookies wandering around looking to exploit incoherent agents.

Better still, however, to focus not on the action of betting, but on inputs to the justification of betting, namely, on the evaluation of prospects. In this I follow other presentations of 'de-pragmatised' DBAs (Armendt 1993; Earman 1992, p. 42; Howson 2000, pp. 124–134; Skyrms 1984, p. 22; though see Maher 1997 for a dissenting voice), all of whom emphasise that non-probabilistic credences involve an inconsistent evaluation of the very same options. Nevertheless, even these authors err in focussing on credences. It may well be that there are good reasons for an agent to evaluate options in an inconsistent way, perhaps because of their practical situation. A risk-averse agent whose neutral price for a bet on a fair coin landing heads is 0.49, and likewise for a bet on it landing tails, inconsistently values the status quo, neutrally valuing the tautology $H \vee \neg H$ at 0.98. If there is pragmatic encroachment on belief, such grounds for incoherent credence might be widespread (Kim 2017; though see Jackson 2019 for an argument that credence isn't encroachable to the same extent as belief). So I think it preferable to focus on the epistemic perspectives that rationalise credence, rather than on realised credences themselves. (How do epistemic perspectives bear on credences? I say a little about that in Section 2.8.)

It is not mandatory to make use of justifications of betting to reveal the structure of rational prospects, though it is a deservedly popular approach. I make use of it here because of its accessibility, but also because it gets at something essential to belief, namely, as Stalnaker puts it, that beliefs are 'representational mental states [and] should be understood primarily in terms of the role that they play in the characterisation and explanation of action' (Stalnaker 1984, p. 4). Betting actions are best explained as normed by appropriately structured epistemic perspectives, and these must be probabilistic if they are to perform this normative function.

A more general approach that still begins with preference over practical options, and thus shares with the DBA an unavoidably decision-theoretic cast, proceeds via *representation theorems*. A representation theorem begins with some axioms taken to govern rational preference and shows that sufficiently rich rational preferences over options can be represented *as if* they involved the maximisation of probabilistic-expected value. Most representation theorems are framed explicitly as accounting for subjective credences (Jeffrey 1983b; Maher 1993; Meacham & Weisberg 2011; Neth 2025; Savage 1972; Titelbaum 2022, pp. 285–309), but can be understood equally as offering norms on those credences, captured by properties of epistemic perspectives. In this case, the idea would be that an epistemic perspective would manifest in ideally rational preference, and must have a probabilistic structure to do so. This kind of approach has no prospect of being 'de-pragmatised', as substantive assumptions about utility must be made.

Another recently popular argument aims to offer purely epistemic grounds for probabilism, on the basis that probabilistic epistemic perspectives are closer to representing how things are – more *accurate* – than non-probabilistic ways of representing an ideal epistemic state, come what may (Joyce 1998; Pettigrew 2016; Titelbaum 2022, pp. 338–361). I discuss this approach in Online Appendix C.

2.6 Conditional Prospects

Frequently, one doesn't want to know only the present prospects of a proposition, the degree of support one's current evidence provides. One wants also to know what bearing hypothetical evidence has on hypotheses one is concerned with: what are the prospects of H, *given* E, where E is not (yet) in evidence? For instance, we might be interested in the support for the hypothesis that some particular die that we haven't yet tossed is fair, given the further potential evidence that it lands '⊞' on 100 consecutive rolls. Presumably that number will be different from the support provided by the current background evidence for its fairness, or from the support provided by the potential evidence that it lands a random mixture of '□', '⊡', ..., '⊞' in roughly equal proportions in 100 rolls. The conditional prospect of H given E relative to some evidential probability Pr is written $\Pr(H \mid E)$.

What is the prospect that both H and E turn out true? Intuitively, it is the proportion among cases where E turns out true that are also cases where H turns out true. Since H may depend in some way on E, this second quantity involves the conditional prospect of H given E. That is, the prospect of the conjunction of H and E is the prospect of H turning out true given E, weighted by the prospect of E turning out true in the first place. The low prospect of my going to the beach *and* getting sunburnt is the prospect that I get sunburnt given I go to the beach (high), weighted by the prospect that I go to the beach (low). This is captured in this rule connecting conditional and unconditional prospects:[3]

Product

$\Pr(H \wedge E) = \Pr(H \mid E)\Pr(E)$. (Jeffrey 2008, p. 12)

There is a betting-price justification of Product, given the natural idea of a conditional bet – one that is called off when E is false (de Finetti 1964/ 1937, p. 146; Howson & Urbach 1993, pp. 81–84). I will not rehearse it here for reasons of space, but none of the issues involved go significantly beyond those canvassed in Section 2.3. It is important to note Product is a purely synchronic claim, and is not a rule about updating.

The Product rule isn't a definition, because the right-hand side mixes conditional and unconditional probability. Nor can it readily be turned into a definition, because we can only rearrange the equation to isolate the term '$\Pr(H \mid E)$' under the assumption that $\Pr(E) > 0$.

To insist that nevertheless conditional probability is to be defined in terms of unconditional probabilities is to adopt the 'ratio analysis', which states that, provided $\Pr(E) > 0$, $\Pr(H \mid E) \overset{\text{def}}{=} \Pr(H \wedge E)/\Pr(E)$. Cases where the ratio analysis gives no guidance are common, since I have not insisted on Regularity (Section 2.4); hence there will be many epistemic perspectives which give no prospect to contingent propositions E. It is a problem for the ratio analysis that it cannot, for example, make sense of the probabilistic independence of the proposition that a fair coin land heads and the

---

[3] Another hypothesis in this area is that conditional support is unconditional support *of a conditional*, that is, that the degree of support of H given E is $\Pr(E \to H)$ for some conditional operator $\to$. This is surprisingly hard to defend (Hájek 2011; Lewis 1976).

proposition that some continuous variable takes a real value (Hájek 2003, p. 286). Because we don't adopt the ratio analysis, we can allow conditional prospects to be defined in many cases where traditional probability theory says they are undefined.

Generally, however, it is only important to consider the conditional support provided by E to H when E itself is genuinely in prospect. If the evidence has no prospect, the support it may or may not provide is (relative to a given epistemic perspective) irrelevant. Of course if one finds oneself frequently confronted by evidence one regarded as having no prospect, that is probably a reason to reconsider the epistemic perspective to which one defers; the space of possibilities it depicts is misaligned with the possibilities being actualised.

A useful clarification is in order here. A conditional degree of support need not be the unconditional degree of support you *would* assign to H if you were to find out that E. It is the degree of support H has, in light of E and your current background evidence. It could be the case that if you were to find out that E, you would revise your background beliefs. Given an epistemic perspective that represented a given die as fair, the conditional degree of support for the die landing '$\square$' given it has landed '$\boxdot$' repeatedly for the past 1,000 rolls is still $1/6$. But if you were to discover that pattern in the actual outcomes, you would be more than reasonable in opting to consider a different epistemic perspective, one that did not have the fairness of the die as part of its background evidence. Perhaps this makes it clear that every evaluation of prospects is really conditional in some sense, the background evidence no less important a factor in the evaluation of an 'unconditional' probability as the explicit proposition E is in the evaluation of conditional probability:

> every evaluation of probability, is conditional; not only on the mentality or psychology of the individual involved, at the time in question, but also, and especially, on the state of information in which he finds himself at that moment. (de Finetti 1974, p. 134)

With conditional degree of support in hand, we can establish some valuable but straightforward results.

Suppose $\mathbf{J} = \{J_1, \ldots, J_n\}$ is a partition of the space of possibilities (defined in Section 2.1), relative to some epistemic perspective. Given any H is logically equivalent to $(H \wedge J_1) \vee \ldots \vee (H \wedge J_n)$, both express the same proposition and have the same probability. Those disjuncts are mutually exclusive because the J_i s are, so Additivity entails $\Pr(H) = \Pr(H \wedge J_1) + \ldots + \Pr(H \wedge J_n)$. Apply the Product rule and we get this basic result:

Total Probability

$$\Pr(H) = \Pr(H \mid J_1)\Pr(J_1) + \ldots + \Pr(H \mid J_n)\Pr(J_n).$$

Another elementary consequence of Product is that $\Pr(H \mid E)\Pr(E) = \Pr(E \mid H)\Pr(H)$. When $\Pr(E) > 0$, this can be rearranged into a theorem that has a prominence belying its obvious proof:

Bayes

$$\Pr(H \mid E) = \frac{\Pr(E \mid H)\Pr(H)}{\Pr(E)}.$$

Applying the theorem of Total probability to '$\Pr(E)$' given a partition including H (e.g., $\{H, H_1, \ldots, H_n\}$), we can reformulate Bayes' theorem:

$$\Pr(H \mid E) = \frac{\Pr(E \mid H)\Pr(H)}{\Pr(E \mid H)\Pr(H) + \Pr(E \mid H_1)\Pr(H_1) + \ldots \Pr(E \mid H_n)\Pr(H_n)}.$$

Bayes' theorem is important because it shows how conditional probabilities $\Pr(H \mid E)$ are fixed by other quantities we often know the value of:

- The *prior* probability of the hypothesis H, $\Pr(H)$;
- The *likelihood* of the evidence given the hypothesis, $\Pr(E \mid H)$;
- The probability of the evidence, $\Pr(E)$, which can also be expressed as the *expected likelihood* of the evidence, given hypotheses spanning the space of possibilities.

The quantity $\Pr(H \mid E)$ is often called the *posterior* probability of the hypothesis.

Here 'prior' and 'posterior' do not refer to temporal priority; $\Pr(H \mid E)$ is evaluated at the same time, and using the same evidential probability Pr, as $\Pr(H)$. There is a very common idea that *if* one is using a probability function to represent an agent's state of mind at some time, *and* that agent was to learn exactly E, then the agent's new state of mind should be $\Pr_E$. The rule of *Conditionalization* says that the relation between this new mental state, taking E into account, and the old mental state, is this: for any H, $\Pr_E(H) = \Pr(H \mid E)$; that is, that the new attitudes should be the old conditional attitudes. In light of this, the genuinely posterior state of mind $\Pr_E(H)$ is equal to a pre-existing conditional attitude, which (by unfortunate extension) is also called the posterior. Conditionalization allows quite radical changes between successive unconditional probabilities, but requires 'rigidity': agreement on conditional probabilities between existing and revised assignments (Weisberg 2009, pp. 14–16).

There is considerable controversy, not unrelated to the earlier discussion of reasoning in Section 1.2, around whether Conditionalization is required as a condition of rationality (Hedden 2015, pp. 29–44; Lewis 1999; Talbott 1991; van Fraassen 1989, pp. 160–182; Williamson 2000, pp. 213–221). My goal is to offer a theory of inductive reasons – not a theory of what one ought to do with them – so I will not pursue this issue (though see Section 3.1). (I will retain the entrenched terms 'prior' and 'posterior'; it would risk unintelligibility to refrain from using them.) Still, the view adopted here that inductive reasons are grounded in a single epistemic perspective fits naturally with conceptions of rationality that take it to be principally a feature of a single 'time slice' of an individual (Hedden 2015, pp. 6–9, 28–55). What matters for rationality is that at each moment a Bayesian agent is probabilistically coherent, adopting a single epistemic perspective that matches one's total evidence. It may not be irrational to have radical discontinuities between successive coherent states of opinion, and there may be no general rule on offer to govern how newly acquired evidence should prompt revisions in the epistemic perspective one comes to adopt, as long as one is rational before and after the revision.

2.7 (Degree of) Evidential Support

With conditional degrees of support, I have finally reached the third key role of epistemic perspectives, namely, capturing the significance of potential evidence for various hypotheses (Section 2.1). That is, an epistemic perspective serves as an inductive framework (Section 1.4), which therefore can be represented by an evidential probability function. Given an epistemic perspective, an unconditional probability already discriminates between hypotheses in light of the background evidence held fixed. Conditional probabilities add a new aspect to that evaluation: they give us some sense of the support various hypotheses would receive from propositions perhaps not yet in evidence, given that we retain the same inductive framework (i.e., standards of evidential significance). So conditional and unconditional probabilities together articulate an 'epistemic standard' that might be deployed in the evaluation of hypotheses (Schoenfield 2012, p. 199). That is, we may finally offer an account of the degree of evidential support and overall evidential support (Section 1.3), relative to an inductive framework:

Degree of Evidential Support

The degree to which E supports H relative to Pr is $\Pr(H \mid E)$. (What Carnap (1962, p. xvi) called *firmness*.)

Overall Support by Evidence

E overall supports H, relative to an epistemic perspective represented by the evidential probability Pr, iff $\Pr(H \mid E) > \Pr(\neg H \mid E)$. (It follows that $\Pr(H \mid E) > 0.5$.)

One limitation of these definitions is that there are cases where $\Pr(H \mid E)$ is high only because $\Pr(H)$ is high. Intuitively, E may have nothing to do with H, or might even be negatively relevant to H, as in many cases where the base rate (prior probability of H) is important (see Section 3.3). This is a significant limitation on the capacity of these definitions to completely track intuition about evidential support.

Accordingly, my focus from now will largely be on the incremental notion of confirmation, rather than on absolute support. This incremental notion is comparative, looking at the difference between the prior support H receives from the background evidence versus the posterior conditional support it receives once E is added to that background evidence. The suggestion is that such comparisons track confirmation or disconfirmation of hypotheses by E. This is the key idea of *Bayesian confirmation theory* – 'Bayesian' because in comparing prior and posterior degrees of support, Bayes' theorem is often used. This is the principal focus of Section 3.

2.8 The Plurality of Epistemic Perspectives

Previously I have only supposed that the numerical prospects assigned to propositions given an epistemic perspective must satisfy the probability axioms. Very many functions do this. So if epistemic perspectives are to justify actual credences (Section 2.2), we shall need some way of deciding which epistemic perspective(s) to adopt as normative for our own individual credences, and what exactly adopting a perspective amounts to.

The second question is easier than the first. To adopt an epistemic perspective is to take its verdicts on support as your own. If Cr is your credence function, representing your degrees of belief, then you've adopted an epistemic perspective Pr iff for any X, $\mathrm{Cr}(X) = \Pr(X)$. The question of whether you *can* adopt an epistemic perspective is another matter. Perhaps epistemic perspectives are too cognitively demanding for us. In that case, adopting an epistemic perspective is an idealisation of rationality, rather than a prescriptive norm (Carr 2021; Staffel 2020).

Return to the first question. You ought not to adopt a perspective that disagrees with you on your total evidence. There are many perspectives meeting this requirement. Can we identify further constraints that allow us to answer our first question as follows: one is doxastically rational in adopting Pr iff Pr is the uniquely permitted epistemic perspective consistent with your total evidence?

Consider an expert weather forecaster, to whom one might defer completely about a limited subject matter, or an omniscient being, to whom one ought to defer completely about everything. One ought, as a seeker after truth, to adopt an (globally or locally) expert epistemic perspective – if only one knew what it was! The literature on *deference* and the epistemology of chance provides a way of proceeding: one's attitude should be one's *expectation* of the expert's attitude (Elga 2007, pp. 478–480; Gaifman 1988; Hall 2004, pp. 100–101; Titelbaum 2022, pp. 133–145). An expected value is a probability-weighted mean value of a quantity. In the much discussed case of chance (Ismael 2008; Joyce 2007; Lewis 1986a), chance deference principles entail (given Total probability from Section 2.6) that one's current attitude to a chancy proposition X should be its expected chance, where each possible value x_i of X's chance is weighted by your judgement of the probability of the hypothesis that x_i turns out to be the actual chance of X.

Since the probabilities of the hypotheses about chance are just as much a matter of epistemic perspective as any other contingent theoretical proposition, it is not plausible that chance deference principles narrow down the class of admissible epistemic perspectives to a uniquely privileged perspective. But deference to chance provides a model for how we might respond to that variety of admissible epistemic perspectives: namely, we ought to set our credence in some hypothesis H equal to the expected support H receives from the various admissible epistemic perspectives under consideration, weighted by our judgements about which epistemic perspectives will turn out to capture the degree to which our evidence supports H.

Mathematically, let there be various epistemic perspectives Pr_i that assign degrees of support p_i to H, and Cr be our actual credence or degree of belief. Next assume that the possible answers to the question *what is the correct degree of support the evidence assigns to H?* form a partition. Let D_i be the proposition that Pr_i captures the correct degrees of support for H in assigning it p_i. Then Total probability will get us this:

$$\mathrm{Cr}(H) = \sum_i \mathrm{Cr}(H \mid D_i)\mathrm{Cr}(D_i),$$

and the epistemic deference principle that $\text{Cr}(H \mid D_i) = p_i$ then yields

$$\text{Cr}(H) = \sum_i p_i \text{Cr}(D_i).$$

This kind of approach works well if there is a single right degree of support or unique evidential probability given a body of evidence – perhaps something like Williamson's 'intrinsic plausibility of hypotheses' (Section 2.4) conditional on our total evidence – and our goal in setting our credences is to best approximate this ideal. Some recent formulations of deference principles for rational belief in fact seem to build in a presupposition of this sort of Uniqueness (Meacham 2019, p. 717; cf. Greco & Hedden 2016). The question of whether Uniqueness is true of evidential probability is the focus of Section 4.

This argument for how to set credences breaks down if there are multiple epistemic perspectives consistent with the evidence. Each embodies some standards for evaluating how the evidence supports hypotheses. There may be no sense in which they are rival accounts of 'the' evidential support relation, and we need not be required to see them as forming a partition of ways this relation could turn out. Their relation to one another may be more like the relation among epistemic perspectives that reflect different bodies of total evidence. There is no one perspective that reflects the evidence one uniquely should have, rather there are many perspectives that may reflect the various bodies of evidence one might have. The question *what is the correct degree to which the evidence supports H* may be in no better shape than the question *what is the correct body of total evidence to draw on when evaluating H*. You draw on the evidence you find yourself having; likewise, perhaps you ought simply to draw on the epistemic standards to which you find yourself subscribing. If that is the case, it is harder to justify adopting as your credence the weighted mean of these various epistemic perspectives. (We can only rationalise expert deference if there is an expert, if there is a fact of the matter about getting the degree of support right that transcends each individual evidential probability function; and in this scenario, there is no single fact of the matter about this.)

Without a unique degree of support, there may be no way to recommend a unique attitude in view of the plurality of epistemic perspectives. That will be bad news for a restrictive epistemology, which aims to tell us what we must do. But if epistemology is *permissive* – in the business of telling us what we *may* do – then a natural idea suggests itself: adopt an epistemic perspective consistent with your total evidence and which reflects your standards for epistemic evaluation. As van Fraassen puts it: 'rationality is only bridled irrationality ... what it is rational to believe includes anything that one is not rationally compelled to disbelieve' (van Fraassen 1989, pp. 171–172). Epistemic rationality requires us to evaluate the prospects of hypotheses. In the absence of constraints that delimit those prospects uniquely, we do what we must by means of what we may: adopt some permissible epistemic perspective. Compare: in unrestricted sections of the Bundesautobahn system, there is no speed limit. While cars must travel at some speed, drivers achieve this requirement by choosing one of the many permissible speeds. This suggests a picture of rational credence in the presence of multiple potentially normative epistemic perspectives:

Permissive Rational Credence

An agent's credence function at a time, Cr, is rational just in case there exists an evidential probability Pr_i such that for any H, $Cr(H) = Pr_i(H)$, where Pr_i agrees with Cr on the total evidence (cf. Climenhaga 2024, p. 6; Meacham 2014, pp. 1186–1189).

Ultimately, then, the question as to which credences are rational amounts to the question of Uniqueness of epistemic perspectives. That, as mentioned earlier, is the focus of Section 4. So far I have identified no reason to accept that there a single perspective compatible with each body of total evidence. Even if there are constraints on perspectives beyond the probability axioms – such as chance deference principles – they appear to leave open many legitimate attitudes to evidential support, as represented in the existence of many evidential probability functions that agree on the total evidence. Before returning to that issue, however, I return in Section 3 to the central project: understanding incremental inductive support using the framework of epistemic perspectives.

3 Bayesian Confirmation Theory

In Section 1.5, we briefly mentioned formal and syntactic approaches to the logic of evidential support, and found them wanting. In Section 2, I suggested that a better approach to evidential support was through the idea of the prospects of hypotheses in light of a body of background evidence and assumptions about the bearing of evidence on hypotheses, jointly encapsulated in the notion of an epistemic perspective, normative for rational credence. I argued that epistemic perspectives ultimately were to be identified with evidential probability functions, and that those functions enable us to define a notion of overall or absolute evidential support of a proposition.

The problem of confirmation, according to Hempel, is 'to characterize, in precise and general terms, the conditions under which a body of evidence can be said to confirm, or to disconfirm, a hypothesis of empirical character' (Hempel 1945a, p. 7). I look at a particular proposal for defining confirmation in terms of the incremental support provided by a piece of evidence, defining it and applying it to some representative cases in Section 3.1. I turn immediately to a famous problem for the Bayesian approach to confirmation, the problem of old evidence (Section 3.2), and argue that it is not an insuperable objection to this approach. Further illustrations of successes of the Bayesian approach in capturing scientific heuristics are given in Sections 3.3 and 3.4, and I examine a famous paradox of confirmation in Section 3.5. The fullest Bayesian treatment of the paradoxes requires a notion of degree of confirmation, and there are a number of inequivalent attempts to measure that, with varying degrees of plausibility; some are introduced and compared in Section 3.6. I conclude by returning to the problem of induction (Section 3.7).

The Bayesian approach, despite its flexibility and adaptability, has not avoided criticism. I will touch on some significant objections as the view is developed, and have hoped to forestall some by design. Some prominent criticisms focus on aspects of some Bayesian views that are not representative of the variant I defend. Consider challenges based on the supposed computational intractability of Bayesian statistics, or the failure of scientists to assign or report probabilities in practice, or the descriptive inaccuracy of the Bayesian picture (Kelly & Glymour 2004, pp. 95–96). These may be telling against personalist Bayesianisms, which take the probabilities involved in support and confirmation as unprocessed credences. It is harder to see how they apply to the degree of support view developed in Section 2.4, which posits evidential probability as a regulative ideal, perhaps not directly implemented in practice.

Other objections are more general; Norton (2011, pp. 400–415) is keen to emphasise ways in which the Bayesian framework appears to require a richer structure on our attitudes than is sometimes justified by the evidence (recall Section 2.8). That could be a problem if the Bayesian is committed to Uniqueness (for then there must be a uniquely rational attitude ungrounded by evidence sufficient to constrain the attitudes uniquely). It appears to be less of a problem for the permissive Bayesian, who allows that there are many legitimate perspectives that can be taken without being uniquely determined – what matter, then, if we are permitted to believe beyond what the evidence demands in these cases too? So this family of objections turns out to connect with what I regard as the principal objection to Bayesianism, the 'problem of the priors'. This objection is the focus of Section 4.

3.1 Incremental Confirmation Defined

A theory of evidential support aims to capture a number of widely shared beliefs about what evidence does for us. For example: that unexpected or novel predictions should favour a hypothesis more than banal or familiar predictions;

or that simpler hypotheses, other things being equal, are favoured by the evidence. Behind these beliefs seems to be a persistent metaphor: evidence as a mass stuff, something that can be gathered and, once collected, *weigh* in favour of a hypothesis and against its rivals. The incremental notion of confirmation aims to capture the idea that each new piece of evidence adds some weight to the scales (or takes some off).

The resultant of all of these pieces of evidence will be a particular degree of evidential support (relative to some background conception of what supports what, of course). Given my conception of degree of support (Section 2.7), it is natural to take the component weight of individual pieces of evidence to be associated with the *changes* in overall degree of support those pieces of evidence produce against a fixed background. If there is some positive weight E contributes to H, we say E *confirms* H. (Whether this positive weight can be *measured* is discussed in Section 3.6.) Confirmation is a three-place relation between some piece of *potential* evidence E, some hypothesis H, and a background probability model. This last is assumed to represent an epistemic perspective and hence to capture both background knowledge and a specific inductive framework, that is, a conception of evidential relevance (Fitelson 2005, p. 391).

Confirmation

E confirms H relative to Pr iff $\Pr(H \mid E) > \Pr(H)$.
E disconfirms H relative to Pr iff $\Pr(H \mid E) < \Pr(H)$.
E is *independent*[4] of *H* relative to Pr iff $\Pr(H \mid E) = \Pr(H)$.

This definition allows us to return to an issue raised back in Section 1.3, the possibility of cases of overall evidential support combined with incremental evidential undermining. In this Bayesian framework, a case like that might involve an epistemic perspective Pr such that H is regarded as more probable than not given some evidence E, that is, $\Pr(H \mid E) > \Pr(\neg H \mid E)$. But it is certainly still possible that $\Pr(H \mid E) < \Pr(H)$ – that is, for E to disconfirm H even while H is on balance supported by E relative to Pr. A case with this structure is discussed in Section 3.3.

This definition is at the heart of *Bayesian confirmation theory* (Earman 1992; Howson & Urbach 1993; Strevens 2006). The term 'Bayesian' is apt because, given this definition of confirmation and Bayes' theorem, E confirms H iff $\frac{\Pr(E \mid H)}{\Pr(E)} > 1$. Given that $\Pr(E)$, the degree to which the background evidence supports the evidence, is constant for any hypotheses we may consider, this result tells us that the confirmation of H by E is driven by the likelihood

---

[4] There are some complications here (Fitelson & Hájek 2014); note too that this notion of probabilistic independence neither implies nor is implied by other sorts of independence such as causal isolation.

$\Pr(E \mid H)$. We are often in a good position to determine this likelihood, because it is often fixed by the content of H itself. Suppose H is a chancy theory, for example. The Principal Principle (Section 2.8) tells us that the likelihood of the evidence on H is its chance of coming about were H the correct theory of E's chance (Strevens 2004, pp. 372–374). Despite the explicit relativisation of evidential support to a probability model, whether a hypothesis H is confirmed turns out to depend on the likelihoods alone, which are in many scientific cases of interest fixed by H itself, and thus common to many epistemic perspectives. What still varies from perspective to perspective is the absolute degree of support for a given hypothesis, whether that hypotheses for example reaches some minimal level of credibility in light of the evidence.

Let's consider a simple example.

Biased Die

Suppose we have background information that leaves open the hypotheses that a die is biased towards '▣' (the chance of '▣' being $1/3$), or that it is fair, and regards these hypotheses as equally supported and exhaustive, so $\Pr(\text{fair}) = \Pr(\text{'▣'-biased})$. No outcomes are yet in evidence. Against this background, consider the proposition that the die lands '▣' 5 times consecutively. That proposition confirms the hypothesis that the die is biased, and disconfirms the hypothesis that the die is fair.

Can Bayesian confirmation theory capture this basic observation about confirmation? Eventually, we might use a theory of confirmation to decide complex cases about which our judgements are unclear, but as usual with a philosophical explication, we need reassurance that it gets the basics right, typically by checking that it reproduces obvious facts about the target relation. In this case, we begin with an appeal to the theorem of Total probability to calculate the prior of E:

$$\begin{aligned} \Pr(E) &= \Pr(E \mid \text{fair})\Pr(\text{fair}) + \Pr(E \mid \text{'▣'-biased})\Pr(\text{'▣'-biased}) \\ &= \frac{1}{6^5} \cdot \frac{1}{2} + \frac{1}{3^5} \cdot \frac{1}{2} \\ &= \frac{1}{15,552} + \frac{1}{486} \approx 0.002122. \end{aligned}$$

Plug this into Bayes' theorem (Section 2.6), and we obtain

$$\begin{aligned} \Pr(\text{fair} \mid E) &\approx 0.0606 \cdot \Pr(\text{fair}) & < \quad \Pr(\text{fair}); \\ \Pr(\text{'▣'-biased} \mid E) &\approx 1.9394 \cdot \Pr(\text{'▣'-biased}) & > \quad \Pr(\text{'▣'-biased}). \end{aligned}$$

So here this proposition confirms the hypothesis of bias, and disconfirms the hypothesis of fairness.

The same sort of reasoning can be applied in less idealised examples. Consider Howson and Urbach's account of Babbage's investigation into the origins of tables of logarithms:

Logarithms

'Babbage ... was interested in whether they derived from the same source or had been worked out independently. Babbage (1827) found the same six errors in all but two and drew the "irresistible" conclusion that, apart from these two, all the tables originated in a common source'. (Howson & Urbach 1993, p. 124)

Howson and Urbach offer this Bayesian reconstruction (following Jevons (1874, pp. 278–279)):

> The theory Copy, which says of some pair of logarithmic tables that they shared a common origin, is moderately likely in view of the immense amount of labour needed to compile such tables *ab initio*, and for a number of other reasons. The alternative, independence theory might take a variety of forms, each attributing different probabilities to the occurrence of errors in various positions in the table. The only one of these which seems at all likely would assign each place an equal probability of exhibiting an error and would, moreover, regard those errors as more-or-less independent. Call this theory Ind and let E^i be the evidence of i common errors in the tables. The posterior probability of Copy is inversely proportional to $\Pr(E^i)$, which, under the assumption of only two rival hypotheses, can be expressed as $\Pr(E^i) = \Pr(E^i \mid \text{Copy})\Pr(\text{Copy}) + \Pr(E^i \mid \text{Ind})\Pr(\text{Ind})$. ... Since Copy entails E^i, $\Pr(E^i) = \Pr(\text{Copy}) + \Pr(E^i \mid \text{Ind})\Pr(\text{Ind})$. The quantity $\Pr(E^i \mid \text{Ind})$ clearly decreases with increasing i. Hence $\Pr(E^i)$ diminishes and approaches $\Pr(\text{Copy})$, as i increases; and so E^i becomes increasingly powerful evidence for Copy, a result which agrees with scientific intuition. (Howson & Urbach 1993, pp. 124–125, notation adjusted)

This reasoning contains two interesting observations. First, the observation that when a hypothesis entails some evidence, $\Pr(E \mid H) = 1$ (by the probability calculus). It follows that $\Pr(H \mid E) = \Pr(H)\frac{1}{\Pr(E)}$ – unless the probability of the evidence is 1, therefore, evidence entailed by a theory supports it. Second, in this case, it is argued that $\Pr(E^i)$ approaches $\Pr(H)$ as the number of common errors goes up (because of the decreasing chance of such a coincidence). So not only does E^i confirm H; the degree of support E^i provides for H approaches 1. We see here not only an invocation of comparative relations of confirmation, but 'absolute' degree of support in light of the evidence. An epistemic perspective with this kind of conception of the available hypotheses, and these ideas about likelihoods informed by background assumptions about chances, supports the proposition that the common errors arise from plagiarism, not luck. Hence any rational attitude adopting such a perspective must inevitably reach the same conclusion.

Recall the observation from Section 1.5 that evidential support is intuitively non-monotonic and intransitive. It is an easy warm up exercise in Bayesian confirmation theory to reproduce these verdicts.

Non-monotonicity

Relative to some Pr, there are bodies of evidence E and F such that E confirms some H but $E \wedge F$ disconfirms H. The ball-drawing example from Section 1.5 exemplifies this structure. Suppose a prior Pr which is uniform over all 101 hypotheses about how many red balls are in the bag of 100 balls: *0 balls are red, 1 ball is red, . . ., 100 balls are red*; this last is our hypothesis H, so $\Pr(H) = 1/101$. Because the evidence F of a black ball drawn from the bag is inconsistent with the hypothesis H that all balls in the bag are red, $\Pr(H \mid E \wedge F) = 0$ (since H must also be inconsistent with any claim that entails F); hence $E \wedge F$ disconfirms H. But E is the evidence of 99 red balls drawn; in light of E, the only live hypotheses are H and *99 balls are red*. $\Pr(H \mid E)$ will therefore be higher than the prior, on any reasonably inductive probability measure (all the probability that was once assigned to the other hypotheses must go to these two, and it is not evidentially required that it all go to the hypothesis that the next ball will be unlike all the others).

Intransitivity

There is a Pr and A, B, C such that $\Pr(B \mid A) > \Pr(B)$, $\Pr(C \mid B) > \Pr(C)$, but $\Pr(C \mid A) \leq \Pr(C)$. Consider a dice rolling case; let A be '□'; let B be the disjunction that the die came up odd, that is, '□ ∨ □ ∨ □' ; let C be the disjunction '□ ∨ □'. The standard die-rolling Pr gives us $\Pr(A) = 1/6$, $\Pr(B) = 1/2$, $\Pr(C) = 1/3$. The relevant conditional probabilities are $\Pr(B \mid A) = 1$ (so A confirms B); $\Pr(C \mid B) = 2/3$ (so B confirms C); but $\Pr(C \mid A) = 0$, so A conclusively disconfirms C.

Many Bayesians are tempted to import their views on diachronic rationality into confirmation theory. From this perspective, 'confirmation' is a thing that happens to a theory when new evidence arrives; the theory is confirmed or disconfirmed as its probability shifts around over time. Most Bayesians accept updating upon receipt of new evidence E goes by Conditionalization, adopting one's old conditional credences given E as one's new 'unconditional' credences. In this case, $\Pr(H \mid E)$ represents the new posterior probability of H; H is confirmed by E if it has come to be more probable once news of E is in. So one sometimes sees Bayesians present confirmation as essentially diachronic:

an experience provides evidence that confirms a hypothesis, for that scientist, if . . . this evidence 'boosts' the scientist's credence in the hypothesis. (Eagle 2011, p. 210)

At the core of modern Bayesianism is a rule for changing the subjective probabilities assigned to hypotheses in the light of new evidence. . . . where $Cr(\cdot)$ is your subjective probability distribution before observing E and $Cr^+(\cdot)$ is your subjective probability distribution after observing E, . . .

$$Cr^+(H) = \frac{Cr(E \mid H)}{Cr(E)} Cr(H).$$

More or less anyone who counts themselves a proponent of BCT thinks that this rule is the rule that governs the way that scientists' opinions should change in the light of new evidence. (Strevens 2004, p. 369; see also Strevens 2006, section 5.1)

But this really runs together two completely separate issues: whether Conditionalization is the right updating rule, and under what synchronic circumstances does one proposition support another. (Recall here Sections 1.2 and 2.6.) It is perfectly possible to endorse the Bayesian account of evidential support while rejecting Conditionalization. Better, then, to interpret the confirmation inequality $Pr(H \mid E) > Pr(H)$ as telling us the current significance of E for H from the single perspective of Pr. That view of evidential significance that may or may not be preserved across successive perspectives, pre- and post-acquisition of E – if the agent adopts a non-rigid update rule, and does not conditionalize on E, they need not in general retain their old view of the bearing of E on H.

3.2 Old Evidence

The foregoing bears on a problem which has been seen by many as a serious challenge to the Bayesian account of confirmation, Glymour's problem of *old evidence*

> Scientists commonly argue for their theories from evidence known long before the theories were introduced. Copernicus argued for his theory using observations made over the course of millennia, not on the basis of any startling new predictions derived from the theory, and presumably it was on the basis of such arguments that he won the adherence of his early disciples. Newton argued for universal gravitation using Kepler's second and third laws, established before the *Principia* was published. The argument that Einstein gave in 1915 for his gravitational field equations was that they explained the

anomalous advance of the perihelion of Mercury, established more than half a century earlier. ... Old evidence can in fact confirm new theory, but according to Bayesian kinematics it cannot. For let us suppose that evidence E is known before theory T is introduced at time t. Because E is known at t, $\text{Pr}_t(E) = 1$ [so] the likelihood of E given T, $\text{Pr}_t(E \mid T)$, is also 1. We then have

$$\text{Pr}_t(T \mid E) = \frac{\text{Pr}_t(T) \times \text{Pr}_t(E \mid T)}{\text{Pr}_t(E)} = \text{Pr}_t(T).$$

The conditional probability of T on E is therefore the same as the prior probability of T: E cannot constitute evidence for T in virtue of the positive relevance condition nor in virtue of the likelihood of E on T. None of the Bayesian mechanisms apply, and if we are strictly limited to them, we have the absurdity that old evidence cannot confirm new theory. (Glymour 1981, pp. 85–86)

As many have noted, the problem is not so much the antiquity of the evidence, as the fact that evidence and hypothesis seem to come in the wrong temporal order. If the age of the evidence were the only problem, we could solve the problem by 'rolling back' to an earlier state of knowledge in which the crucial evidence isn't included – this seems to be what Howson and Urbach have in mind when they say '$\text{Pr}(H)$ measures your belief in a hypothesis *when* you do not know the evidence' (1993, p. 117, my emphasis). But Climenhaga (2024, section 3) sets up a simple example in which a piece of evidence is acquired, then some crucial information about the probability distribution over hypotheses is acquired, and then a posterior probability over hypotheses is calculated. Roll back the credence to before the acquisition of the evidence, and one also loses the distributional information. There was never, in his case, a state of belief that represented the background against which this evidence is confirmatory in the way it appears to be.

Introduced like that, old evidence is not a problem for the Bayesian view I have presented, which involves no 'kinematic'/diachronic element. Though I follow the Bayesian literature in talking of confirmation of hypotheses by evidence, and use the suggestive variable 'E', I explicitly reject the idea that confirmation occurs when evidence is newly acquired (Carnap 1962, p. 468; Hempel 1945a, section 6). There is no sense in which the evidence considered with respect to confirmation has to be collected at all. Recall my discussion in Section 2.1; an epistemic perspective is associated with some body of total evidence, some body of propositions (it turned out) that are assigned probability 1 by the perspective. Nothing temporal is involved in this characterisation. Utilise an epistemic perspective including E as evidence, and it won't confirm anything; utilise an epistemic perspective not including E, and it may well have confirmatory power. This is independent of when E is gathered, or even if it is gathered. The incremental confirmation relation informs us of the evidential bearing of one proposition on another, relative to an epistemic perspective; neither needs to be 'evidence' in a folk or philosophical sense for this evidential bearing to obtain. Rather, E is some claim that might bear on H – perhaps H predicts it, or some rival of H predicts it – and we wish to evaluate its significance, relative to some perspective embodying some appropriate principles of evidential bearing.

To do this, of course, one must make use of an epistemic perspective according to which there is some bearing of E on H. Glymour's argument certainly emphasises that a perspective that assigns probability 1 to E is not appropriate for this purpose. Nor for that matter is one that assigns probability 1 to H, which would then be incapable of being confirmed. Nothing in the framework I've presented requires us to make such inappropriate choices; but nothing tells us which choices to make, either. So the *synchronic* problem of old evidence is to give defensible guidance about which epistemic perspective we ought to consider when we evaluate confirmation of hypotheses by claims which are already in evidence for us.

One obvious candidate is clearly excluded because it will simply reinscribe the problem of old evidence. This is the proposal that we ought to evaluate claims of confirmation relative to an epistemic perspective we've adopted. My account of adoption in Section 2.8 guaranteed that anything in evidence for us is assigned probability 1 by any adoptable perspective. Hence the problem of old evidence shows that even at a fixed point in time there is no single body of background evidence: the background evidence relevant to the adoption of an epistemic perspective is the evidence possessed by the adopting agent, which may be different than the body of evidence against which that very same agent assessed claims of confirmation. A theory of confirmation is quite distinct from a theory of individual belief, as Glymour (1981, p. 74) pointed out; this unworkable proposal would collapse them.

Some suggest simply removing E from the background evidence, and evaluating all confirmation claims relative to an epistemic perspective that treats that background (mutilated, from our perspective) as its total evidence:

> One answer – and I think the correct one – to Glymour's nasty problem . . . is to deny that when assessing support according to the difference between $\Pr(H \mid E)$ and $\Pr(H)$, the probabilities should be relativized to K; rather they should *always* be relativized to $K\backslash\{E\}$ . . . And why? The answer is straightforward. When you ask yourself how much support E gives H, you are plausibly asking how much a knowledge of E *would* increase the credibility of H, which is the same thing as asking how much H boosts the credibility of H relative to what *else* you currently know. The 'what else' is just $K\backslash\{E\}$. (Howson 1991, p. 548)

The proposal is an example of a more general class of *counterfactual* theories, those that evaluate the confirmatoriness of E with respect to how much E 'would increase' the credibility of H against a counterfactual background, what we would have known had we not known E. Howson's approach is, in effect, that we would have known everything but E. Howson's suggestion seems to give two sorts of incorrect predictions about confirmation.

The first is this. Sometimes a generalisation is confirmed by its instances (Section 3.5), and, in the Baconian fashion (Bacon 2000/1620), may only be proposed after diligent apian collection of facts. We know that there is a point at which confirmatory returns to repeated experiments must diminish to zero (Howson & Urbach 1993, p. 120). In such a case, subtracting any particular instance from background knowledge leaves many similar instances, and no confirmation by that instance. The same is true, clearly, for every instance – so no instance confirms. Howson seems blasé about this (1991, p. 550). Yet intuitively each instance may be highly confirmatory were *none* of the similar instances present, and our instincts in particular cases go with this latter observation. In this case, the counterfactual about what the Baconian would have believed had they not believed E seems to give us $K\backslash\{E\}$, as Howson claims, but that seems to be the wrong body of background evidence to use in evaluating confirmation.

In that case, the counterfactual yields the 'wrong' body of background evidence to assess confirmation. There are other cases in which Howson's counterfactual account yields the right background, but predicts the wrong epistemic perspective: it not only subtracts E from the background knowledge, it also shifts us to an epistemic perspective in which evaluations of the bearing of E on H are different. This is the second sort of incorrect prediction Howson's account makes. Maher gives this example:

> Mr. Schreiber is the author of novels that are popular (P) though it is important to him that he is making important contributions to literature (I). Schreiber basks in his success, taking his popularity to be evidence of the importance of his work; that is, he takes P to confirm I. ... many aspiring serious novelists whose work is unpopular tend to rationalize their failure by supposing that the public taste is so depraved that nothing of true value can be popular. ... if Schreiber did not know of his own work's popularity, he too would share this opinion ... [That is,] were he not to know P, he would have a probability function Pr such that $\Pr(I \mid P) \leq \Pr(I)$. (Maher 1996, p. 156)

What we want is something like this: a surgical modification of our current adopted epistemic perspective that preserves our dispositions to evaluate the bearing of E on H, while removing E and evidence substantially similar to E to predict the right judgements about confirmation. That suggests the following proposal (Eells & Fitelson 2000, pp. 667–669; Jeffrey 2008, pp. 44–47; Meacham 2016, pp. 461–462):

Ur-Probability

In an assessment of confirmation, the probability function Pr must be such that

1. There is some *ur*-probability Pr_0 that does not assign unconditional probability 1 to any proposition that confirms or disconfirms H, such that, where V is one's current total evidence, $Pr_0(\cdot \mid V)$ is an adoptable epistemic perspective;
2. There exists some 'contextually determined background evidence' B (Meacham 2016, p. 462), such that $B \subseteq V$ and $Pr(\cdot) = Pr_0(\cdot \mid B)$.

This proposal, unlike Howson's, doesn't require the determinacy of any counterfactual claim about what attitudes we might have had supposing we had different evidence. The relativity to background evidence is made explicit in a way that permits us to remove more than E if needed; but we preserve judgements of evidential bearing, by requiring that the *ur*-probability be one that could end up with an adoptable evidential probability.

The role of background is vital, because of a further problem with Howson's approach I have not yet noted: that very often, old news is no news. The example of perihelion of Mercury is rather unusual; many pieces of evidence have no confirmatory value at all, being so thoroughly absorbed into the perspectives on the world that no context renders them as foreground. It is perfectly reasonable to think that the fact that something exists, for example, is part of my total evidence, and forms part of the base of support for various hypotheses I entertain. It would be very strange to think of this fact as confirming any hypotheses, since no live hypothesis is incompatible with it. So it is important to note that our proposal does not require that $E \notin B$, though obviously in many cases it will be included.

This proposal tells us that whether, and to what extent, E confirms H is relative to background assumptions in two ways. First, it is relative to some assumption about evidential bearing, encoded in the prior conditional probabilities. Second, it is relative to some selection of background evidence. Neither of these relativities collapses into one another. If the thesis of Uniqueness is true (Sections 2.8 and 4), then there is only one legitimate perspective on evidential bearing, and yet there remain many possible selections of background evidence. On the other hand, one could accept permissivism about what bears on what, and think that epistemology proper must always consider the current total evidence in evaluating the justification of belief. The problem of old evidence brings the second sort of relativity to the background into a clear view: even at a given point in time, there is no single body of evidence that it is pertinent to confirmation.

Can we be more specific about how context selects background evidence? General Gricean principles governing conversation are more helpful here than special-purpose considerations about theory testing (Grice 1989). Rather than multiply theoretical posits beyond necessity, I will simply identify the background evidence with a conversational context: for example, that of a discussion between scientists about the merits of a theory, in person, or in the pages of the journals. (It could even be a private conversation the individual has with themselves.) A context, for Stalnaker, comprises 'the body of information that is presumed, at that point, to be common to the participants in the discourse' (Stalnaker 1999/1998, p. 98). There are a couple of ways to think about old evidence given this. One is to note the diversity of the scientific community; perhaps the scholarly community isn't all of a uniform opinion about the perihelion of Mercury, for example. In that case this old evidence, though known to some, cannot be common ground, and hence will not be included in the background evidence.

More interesting is a second approach. Suppose you and I are talking about a brand new hire at our company, Jack, with whom I've just had an unpleasant interaction. I ask 'why is Jack so irritable?', and you say, 'He's just stopped smoking'. I don't know Jack at all; it is not common ground to us that Jack was previously a smoker. The sentence however *presupposes* that Jack used to smoke – saying it is only legitimate on that assumption, so perhaps it ought to misfire if that assumption isn't common ground. That it does not is, Lewis suggests, due to *accommodation*:

> If at time *t* something is said that requires presupposition *P* to be acceptable, and if *P* is not presupposed just before *t*, then – *ceteris paribus* and within certain limits – presupposition *P* comes into existence at *t*. (Lewis 1979, p. 340)

That we accommodate the conversational moves of other speakers, I contend, also makes sense of conversational contributions that force the *retraction* of items in the common ground. Because the common ground is a set of assumed propositions, any conversational contribution that expands the possibilities under consideration can remove propositions from common ground. This, Lewis thinks, is how the sceptical argument works. What we know is what holds in all possibilities consistent with our evidence. If some new possibility is raised to salience, then our evidence is revised – weakened – so as not to exclude the new possibility. This is Lewis' 'Rule of Attention' (Lewis 1996, p. 559): when you attend to some new possibility, you do not ignore it, and hence do not know it not to obtain, and hence it can no longer be common ground. This also looks like a kind of accommodation: 'possibly, P' presupposes that $\neg P$ is not in the common ground; if a speaker says it, we accommodate their utterance by ensuring that $\neg P$ *isn't* in the common ground. (The same is true if a speaker says P which we had been assuming was common ground. Stalnaker says 'it is in general required that the proposition which is expressed by the use of a sentence in a context *not* be presupposed in that context' (1973, p. 454); if this general requirement is imposed, to say P demands – and automatically receives – accommodation if your conversational partners were assuming $\neg P$.)

These sorts of examples, I contend, might play a role in confirmation by old evidence. Ask questions about confirmation, such as 'is the theory of relativity supported by the evidence?', 'does the geological record confirm Uniformitarianism?', and so on, and we trigger an accommodatory shift to a context in which the common ground includes neither evidence nor hypothesis. If it did, those questions would generally be trivially answerable by the questioner already. A broadly Gricean account then says: the questioner must not be presupposing what they are asking about, on the assumption that they are being cooperative. And then the context shifts to accommodate the speaker's not presupposing E by ensuring that $\neg E$ becomes (again) a live possibility, against which conversational background we can then evaluate $\Pr(H \mid E)$ so that it is a non-trivial question whether it exceeds $\Pr(H)$.

There is doubtless more to say about how background context selects a relevant body of evidence against which confirmation is evaluated. But saying it is not specifically the job of a logic of confirmation. And what has been said suffices, I think, to fend off the challenge of old evidence.

3.3 Base Rates

Some students of the scientific method analyse the cases from Section 3.1 slightly differently. They are sympathetic to the idea that probability is central to evidential support. But they are suspicious of the apparent arbitrariness that goes into selecting a particular epistemic perspective to assign prior probabilities to evidence and hypothesis (Royall 1997, p. xiii), and unconvinced by any of the proposals I will discuss later (Section 4) to allow the background evidence to constrain that selection uniquely. However these philosophers are impressed with the apparent objectivity of the likelihoods that play such an important role in confirmation. They want to rest their whole account of confirmation on likelihoods, and set aside prior probabilities of evidence and hypothesis as much as they can. I take a closer look at these *Likelihoodists* (Milne 1996; Royall 1997; Sober 1994) in Online Appendix D. The evidential probability framework ameliorates to a certain extent this Likelihoodist charge of 'subjectivity': there is nothing subjective about confirmation relative to a probability model.

This Likelihoodist impulse should probably be resisted because there are cases where the prior probability of hypotheses seems to be confirmationally significant. Let's consider a simplified example.

Mammogram

Mary, a woman aged 47, attends her annual mammogram. Mary has no other symptoms, but while she is waiting for the initial results, she worries: what if there is something abnormal on the scan? Won't that be evidence of cancer?

Mary has some reason to worry, but perhaps not as much as we might antecedently think. Suppose we consider an epistemic perspective that incorporates information about the error rates for mammograms for women in Mary's situation. Table 2 shows some broadly indicative aggregate statistics about mammogram results, though the actual data is rather complex.

The true positive rate, otherwise known as the *sensitivity* of a test, is the likelihood of an abnormal mammogram given cancer. Given these statistics,

$$\Pr(A \mid C) = \frac{\text{TP}}{\text{TP} + \text{FN}} = \frac{8529}{9812} = 0.869.$$

The true negative rate, or *specificity*, is the likelihood of a normal mammogram given that the test subject doesn't have cancer:

$$\Pr(\neg A \mid \neg C) = \frac{\text{TN}}{\text{TN} + \text{FP}} = \frac{1,486,553}{1,672,692} = 0.889.$$

Accordingly, the likelihood of an abnormal mammogram given no cancer is $\Pr(A \mid \neg C) = 1 - \Pr(\neg A \mid \neg C) = 0.111$ (cf. Hendrick & Helvie 2011, p. W113).

These likelihoods tell us about the test: how reliable is it? Because of how rare cancer actually is, the reliability of the test is not especially informative for

Table 2 Aggregate test results for 1,682,504 mammograms 2007–2013 (Lehman et al. 2017, p. 53, table 2).

	Normal mammogram	Abnormal mammogram	Total
No cancer	1,486,553 (TN)	186,139 (FP)	1,672,692 ($\neg C$)
Cancer	1,283 (FN)	8,529 (TP)	9,812 (C)
Total	1,487,836 ($\neg A$)	194,668 (A)	1,682,504

the patient. We can see this in the overall support that an abnormal test result provides to the hypothesis of cancer. On the data in Table 2, the cancer rate among all screenings is $\Pr(C) = 9,812/1,682,504 \approx 0.006$. This is the *base rate*. Bayes' theorem tells us that the predictive value of a positive test result is not the sensitivity of the test, but rather the probability of cancer given an abnormal result:

$$\Pr(C \mid A) = \frac{\Pr(A \mid C)\Pr(C)}{\Pr(A \mid C)\Pr(C) + \Pr(\neg A \mid C)\Pr(\neg C)}$$

$$= \frac{0.869 \cdot 0.006}{0.869 \cdot 0.006 + 0.111 \cdot 0.994} \approx 0.045.$$

In effect, this posterior probability balances the sensitivity of the test against the number of opportunities for even a reliable test to go wrong, indicated by the high base rate for no cancer. So while we see incremental confirmation of cancer from the abnormal result, we see that the degree to which the total evidence supports a cancer diagnosis is very low.

The Bayesian approach makes it easy to incorporate the evidential relevance of the base rate. In my framing, the base rate provides a constraint on the bearing of statistical evidence about test reliability. In a world where the base rate of H is low, a positive result on a sensitive test is good evidence for H. In a world where the base rate of H is high, that same positive result need not be good evidence for H. The Bayesian approach incorporates both a story about confirmation, and a story about how evidential relevance is fixed by background perspective, and cases where base rates are significant show that understanding the impact of evidence needs both. Accounts which neglect the base rate – including Likelihoodism, significance testing, and frequentist statistics – do not provide an account of evidential relevance, and suffer in comparison to the unified picture provided by Bayesianism.

3.4 The Scientific Method

That Bayesian confirmation theory can reproduce judgements about evidential support in particular cases is promising. That it has a natural and unified account of the relevance of base rates is also promising. But we also have an existing body of principles and heuristics that together form a proto-theory of evidential support, embedded in the practice of science. The success of science indicates some value to these truisms comprising the 'scientific method', so Bayesian accounts of evidential support are vindicated when they are able to reconstruct and systematise ideal scientific practice. As Earman notes, 'an adequate account of confirmation is not under obligation to give an unqualified endorsement to all such truisms' (Earman 1992, p. 77), but ideally, it should explain the success of those we should endorse. For reasons of space, my discussion here will be partial. The topic of Bayesian philosophy of science is treated extensively elsewhere (Earman 1992, pp. 63–86; Horwich 1982, pp. 100–130; Howson & Urbach 1993, pp. 117–164; Schupbach 2022).

Consider the role of *refutation* in scientific inference. When a theory makes a determinate prediction (relative as always to background assumptions) which is not borne out in experiment, that is often taken to decisively undermine the prospects of that theory. For example, the simplest aether theory of the propagation of light was decisively undermined by the outcome of the Michelson–Morley experiment, which did not observe the predicted difference in the speed of light in perpendicular directions, while background assumptions excluded rival aether-preserving explanations.[5] This sort of case is central enough to scientific practice that Popper (1959) was able to make it the centrepiece of his 'falsificationist' approach to theory choice. The correctness of this judgement is supported by a Bayesian model. When H determinately predicts E, relative to background assumptions, that is reflected in the likelihood $\Pr(\neg E \mid H) = 0$ (there is no prospect of E's falsity). In that case,

$$\Pr(H \mid \neg E) = \Pr(\neg E \mid H)\frac{\Pr(H)}{\Pr(\neg E)} = 0.$$

So falsifying evidence conclusively undermines a hypothesis. The displayed equation shows that, in general, the degree of support of a hypothesis by evidence is proportional to increasing likelihood, the limit case being where H entails E.

There is an asymmetry here (which Popper's view may mesh with), in that evidence that a theory predicts we *won't* see provides conclusive disconfirmation, while evidence that a theory predicts we *will* see does not yield conclusive confirmation. (H is conclusively confirmed by E only when E excludes $\neg H$, relative to background knowledge.) But in those cases where a hypothesis predicts some proposition, so that $\Pr(E \mid H) = 1$, we see a degree of support

---

[5] The role of background assumptions is vital; one can always, as the Quine–Duhem thesis would have it, save a theory by rejecting an auxiliary assumption. Normally the relative confirmation and disconfirmation of theory and auxiliary will depend on the relative impact of the refuting evidence on the posterior probability of each; it is possible to model, in a fairly robust way, historically plausible choices of epistemic perspective that reproduce widely accepted judgements about when theories are refuted and when auxiliaries are to be rejected (Dorling 1979; Strevens 2001).

of H by E that is equal to $\frac{\Pr(H)}{\Pr(E)}$. Firstly, note that if we hold the prior probability of H fixed, the more improbable E is, the more support it provides for H. This gives us the value of *surprising evidence*: other things being equal, antecedently unexpected evidence has greater evidential impact for the hypotheses that predict it than evidence we'd expect anyway.[6]

Secondly, note that $\Pr(H \mid E) = \frac{\Pr(H)}{\Pr(E)}$ entails $\Pr(H \mid E) > \Pr(H)$: entailed evidence invariably confirms, just as the Entailment condition would have it (Section 1.4). This prompts us to briefly revisit Hempel's theory of confirmation (Section 1.5). Hempel endorsed this principle, which superficially seems akin to the Entailment Principle:

Special Consequence
If an observation report confirms a hypothesis H, then it also confirms every consequence of H. (Hempel 1945b, p. 103).

This principle has intuitive counterexamples, and a Bayesian account of confirmation explains why. Here is an example:

> There is a jar of ten marbles in front of me, five of which were made in Canada and five of which were made in the United States. Of the five marbles made in Canada, four are white and one is red. Of the five marbles made in the United States, all five are red. I am blindfolded, and a friend picks a marble at random from the bag and calls the selected marble 'marble X'. He tells me that marble X is red; let E be 'X is red', H_1 be 'X is the (unique) red marble from Canada', and H_2 be 'X is from Canada'. (Kotzen 2012, p. 63)

H_2 is a logical consequence of H_1. The intuitive verdict is that while E supports H_1 (along with every other hypothesis that the marble is one of the red ones), it doesn't support H_2 (since the typical Canadian marble isn't red). A Bayesian treatment endorses these verdicts. The evidence E supports H_1: $\Pr(H_1) = 1/10 < 1/6 = \Pr(H_1 \mid E)$. But E disconfirms H_2: $\Pr(H_2) = 1/2 > 1/6 = \Pr(H_2 \mid E)$. (This case also provides another counterexample to Hempel's Consistency Condition: E confirms both H_1 and $\neg H_2$, even though they are inconsistent with one another.)

It appears to be a methodological rule that, other things being equal, the more *diverse* the sources of evidence for one's theory, the more strongly confirmed

---

[6] An example discussed by Jeffrey (2008, section 2.3): In 1846, the French astronomer Leverrier, on the basis of various irregularities in Uranus' motion and Newtonian mechanics (call this H), predicted the existence, and orbit, of a large, extra-Uranian planet. This planet was subsequently found (call this E) and named 'Neptune'. The prior credence in E is $1/180$ – the probability of choosing a point on a circle to within 1 degree (since all the planets are found in the ecliptic, and that was the accuracy of Leverrier's prediction). $\Pr(E \mid H) \approx 1$; so $\Pr(H \mid E) \approx \Pr(H)/\Pr(E) \approx 180 \cdot \Pr(H)$: a strong confirmatory boost for Newtonian mechanics. This kind of pattern is seen also in the Babbage example from Section 3.1.

that theory is. This can be captured in this maxim: *A theory which makes predictions in a number of disparate and seemingly unconnected areas is more confirmed by that evidence than is a theory which is confirmed by predictions only about a narrow and circumscribed range.* This maxim is also part of the grounds for recommending random sampling in population inference. The Bayesian insight is that diverse evidence is not internally correlated (Howson & Urbach 1993, p. 160; Steel 1996, pp. 667–668). If, for example, the hypothesis is that all swans are white, then swans collected from different countries would, if white, provide better evidence for the hypothesis than swans collected from the same pond, as we know that if one swan on a pond is white, it is much more likely to be related to other swans in its pond, and those are more likely therefore to be white. If the hypothesis is false, correlations between diverse evidence are more coincidental than correlations between similar evidence. (From a falsificationist perspective, diverse predictions pose a more severe test to the proposal that our hypothesis is false.)

Again focussing on the case where hypothesis predicts evidence with (near) certainty, if the evidence is diverse, it consists of at least two propositions, E_1 and E_2, such that truth of one is not positively relevant to the truth of the other, *if the hypothesis in question is false.* (If it is true, then the evidence is all true, so correlated.) So E_1 and E_2 are diverse *relative to H* iff the likelihood $\Pr(E_1 \wedge E_2 \mid \neg H)$ is low, or at least if it is not greater than the product of the individual likelihoods $\Pr(E_1 \mid \neg H)\Pr(E_2 \mid \neg H)$.

The likelihood ratio $\frac{\Pr(E_1 \wedge E_2 \mid \neg H)}{\Pr(E_1 \wedge E_2 \mid H)}$ features in this formulation of Bayes' theorem:

$$\Pr(H \mid E) = \frac{\Pr(H)}{\Pr(H) + \frac{\Pr(E_1 \wedge E_2 \mid \neg H)}{\Pr(E_1 \wedge E_2 \mid H)}\Pr(\neg H)}.$$

If the hypothesis H predicts both E_1 and E_2, then the likelihood $\Pr(E_1 \wedge E_2 \mid H)$ is close to one. The likelihood ratio is therefore close to $\Pr(E_1 \wedge E_2 \mid \neg H)$. Substitute this in:

$$\Pr(H \mid E_1 \wedge E_2) \approx \frac{\Pr(H)}{\Pr(H) + \Pr(E_1 \wedge E_2 \mid \neg H)\Pr(\neg H)}.$$

But if E_1 and E_2 are diverse (uncorrelated) evidence, then so long as neither is certain given $\neg H$, this guarantees that the term $\Pr(E_1 \wedge E_2 \mid \neg H) < 1$, and hence that $\Pr(H \mid E_1 \wedge E_2) > \Pr(H)$.

Moreover, the more surprising each piece of independent evidence is, and the more we have, the more confirmatory diverse evidence is. As we consider additional pieces of diverse evidence,

$$\lim_{i \to \infty} \Pr(E_1 \wedge E_2 \wedge \ldots \wedge E_i \mid \neg H) = 0,$$

hence $\Pr(H \mid E_1 \wedge E_2 \wedge \ldots \wedge E_i)$ tends to 1. This result requires independent evidence; correlated evidence doesn't have increasing confirmatory impact the more of it one collects.

We must bear in mind as always that judgements of diversity are relative to theoretical background:

> the notion of variety of evidence has to be relativized to the background assumptions K, but there is no more than good scientific common sense here, since, for example, before the scientific revolution the motions of the celestial bodies seemed to belong to a different variety than the motions of terrestrial projectiles, whereas after Newton they seem like peas in a pod. (Earman 1992, p. 79)

Here is another methodological rule: other things being equal, science prefers naturally arising theories to ad hoc ones designed to predict the same evidence. Suppose a hypothesis, springing unbidden to the scientific mind, entails a certain piece of evidence; and another hypothesis is then designed to mimic the success of the first theory, entailing the evidence by construction. An example is provided by van Fraassen:

> It is part of [Newton's] theory that there is such a thing as Absolute Space, that absolute motion is motion relative to Absolute Space, ... He offered in addition the *hypothesis* (his term) that the centre of gravity of the solar system is at rest in Absolute Space. But as he himself noted, the appearances would be no different if that centre were in any other state of constant relative motion. This is the case for two reasons: differences between true motions are not changed if we add a constant factor to all velocities; and force is related to changes in motion (accelerations) and to motion directly. (van Fraassen 1980, p. 46)

Consider Newton's theory N, and the constructed alternative $N + \vec{v}$, that the centre of gravity of the solar system has constant absolute velocity $\vec{v}$. These theories will make the same empirical predictions, so from the point of view of evidence they are indistinguishable. Yet one might think, Newton's theory is clearly to be preferred to each of the arbitrary variants. (Perhaps an even better theory is neo-Newtonian, doing away with absolute space altogether.)

This sort of case has been raised as an objection to Likelihoodism (cf. Norton 2011, pp. 420–22). Considering only the likelihoods of hypotheses, what resources does the Likelihoodist have to explain our distaste for ad hoc hypotheses? N and

$N + \vec{v}$ both entail the evidence, so the likelihoods are the same, and there the Likelihoodist account stops. To explain this methodological preference, we cannot appeal to the likelihoods alone, but must also appeal to the disparity in prior probability between the antecedently plausible Newtonian theory N and the antecedently implausible $N + \vec{v}$. One might offer all sorts of explanations for why this prior disparity exists – perhaps Newton's theory is simpler, more natural, and less arbitrary – but that it exists and drives judgements of confirmation is undeniable. The Bayesian view of ad hoc theories then is that they may have some credibility, and may be supported by evidence, but that generally the fact that they are cooked up to preserve the empirical predictions prompts people to assign them low probability:

> people often respond immediately with incredulity, even derision, on first hearing certain *ad hoc* hypotheses. . . . it is . . . likely that they are reacting to what they see as the utter implausibility of the hypothesis. (Howson & Urbach 1993, p. 158)

There is one kind of case that may trouble the Bayesian: when the ad hoc hypothesis is cooked up to be entailed by the original hypothesis. Suppose $N^\dagger$ is stipulated to be the theory, 'N or the empirical appearances are just as if N'. Any evidence E entailed by N is also entailed by $N^\dagger$; since N entails $N^\dagger$, $\Pr(N^\dagger) \geq \Pr(N)$. So we can't appeal to the implausibility of ad hoc rivals to explain our decided preference for N; if N is probable enough to be believed, so is $N^\dagger$. In this case, we might need to appeal to another broadly Gricean principle: that our conversational contributions be as informative as they can be, subject to other conversational norms. N is more informative than $N^\dagger$. Perhaps our preference for N is about what we should *say* we believe, more than about what is credible.

3.5 The Ravens Paradox

The role of background assumptions is also vital for the Bayesian treatment of Hempel's 'paradox of the ravens'. Here is how Hempel introduces the problem:

> if a is both a raven and black, then a certainly confirms S_1: '$\forall x(\text{Raven}(x) \rightarrow \text{Black}(x))$'; and if d is neither black nor a raven, d certainly confirms S_2: '$\forall x\left(\neg\,\text{Black}(x) \rightarrow \neg\,\text{Raven}(x)\right)$'. Let us now combine this simple stipulation with the Equivalence Condition [(that evidence confirms logically equivalent hypotheses equally)]: Since S_1 and S_2 are equivalent, d is confirming also for S_1; and thus, we have to recognize as confirming for S_1 any object which is neither black nor a raven. Consequently, any red pencil, any green leaf, and yellow cow, etc., becomes confirming evidence for the hypothesis that all ravens are black. (Hempel 1945a, p. 14, notation modified)

This conclusion appears implausible. Our judgement grows 'out of the feeling that the hypothesis that all ravens are black is about ravens, and not about non-black things, nor about all things' (Hempel 1945a, p. 17). The conclusion Hempel draws is that Nicod's Condition should be rejected in light of its 'several deficiencies' (Hempel 1945a, p. 22).

Clearly, the Bayesian will accept the Equivalence Condition; evidential support relates propositions, given an epistemic perspective, and logically equivalent propositions are identical. Existing counterexamples show that Nicod's Condition isn't invariably correct (Section 1.5). But we cannot conclude that instances *never* confirm generalisations; that would be overkill as a response to the paradox. The Bayesian has an account here; indeed, they have two. For there is an account of the circumstances under which Nicod's Condition fails; and there is an account of how to dissolve the paradox, even when Nicod's Condition obtains.

How does the Bayesian account for the failures of Nicod's Condition? By appeal to background knowledge. Recall Good's (1967, p. 322) example from Section 1.5 of the two worlds, one with relatively few crows, all of which are black, versus the other with many crows, one of which is white. Suppose our background evidence is symmetrical between the two possible worlds, so we adopt an epistemic perspective in which $\Pr(H) = 0.5$. The evidence E is that a black crow is selected at random: $\Pr(E \mid H) = \frac{100}{1,000,100} \approx 0.0001$, while $\Pr(E \mid \neg H) = \frac{1,000}{1,001,001} \approx 0.001$.[7] Hence $\Pr(E) \approx 0.5 \cdot 0.0001 + 0.5 \cdot 0.001 \approx 0.00055$, and $\Pr(H \mid E) \approx 0.009 < \Pr(H)$. So we see evidence that disconfirms the hypothesis even while being an instance of it. This example is rather confected, but more realistic examples with the same structure are available. Suppose an epidemiologist is thinking about a virulent illness, endemic overseas, which they are worrying may have begun to take root in their community. The scenarios they are considering are two: there is no reservoir of disease in their community, and there is a significant hitherto-undiagnosed population of positive cases. They get word of a positive case recently diagnosed, an instance of the generalisation 'all cases of the disease have been identified'. But of course, this positive case is conclusive evidence that the disease is in the community, and hence conclusive evidence against the truth of the generalisation.

The counterexamples to Nicod's Condition have the distinctive feature that encountering certain instances of the generalisation indicates its falsity, relative to background knowledge. In many cases, however, whether we encounter an F is independent of any generalisation about the qualities of Fs. Consider such a case (Earman 1992, p. 72; Howson & Urbach 1993, p. 127;

---

[7] Here notice we must use the total evidence acquired; the evidence is not merely that there is a black raven, but that a black raven was the result of a random selection – it is clearly that latter aspect of the evidence that renders it so unlikely in the world where the generalization is true.

see also Hosiasson-Lindenbaum 1940). Let the proposition that an entity a is encountered be part of the background knowledge, and then let R be the proposition 'a is a raven', and B the proposition 'a is black'. That a black raven is encountered is then $R \wedge B$, a non-black, non-raven encountered being $\neg B \wedge \neg R$. Let A be the hypothesis 'all ravens are black'. $R \wedge B$ confirms A iff $\Pr(A \mid R \wedge B)/\Pr(A) > 1$.

Rearranging an instance of Bayes' theorem gives us

$$\frac{\Pr(A \mid R \wedge B)}{\Pr(A)} = \frac{\Pr(R \wedge B \mid A)}{\Pr(R \wedge B)}.$$

If all ravens are black, then a's being a raven guarantees it to be black: so $\Pr(B \mid A \wedge R) = 1$. Hence $\Pr(R \wedge B \mid A) = \Pr(R \mid A)$; and the independence of encountering a raven from the hypotheses about the characteristics of ravens entails that $\Pr(R \mid A) = \Pr(R)$. So

$$\frac{\Pr(A \mid R \wedge B)}{\Pr(A)} = \frac{\Pr(R)}{\Pr(R \wedge B)}.$$

Similar reasoning will show that

$$\frac{\Pr(A \mid \neg B \wedge \neg R)}{\Pr(A)} = \frac{\Pr(\neg B)}{\Pr(\neg B \wedge \neg R)}.$$

Turning now to the probability of the evidence, suppose we have various hypotheses about the proportion of ravens that are black. Let F_i state that the frequency of black things among the ravens is $100i$ per cent; thus $A = F_1$. The probability, given one has encountered something, that it is a black raven is the probability of encountering a raven, multiplied by the probability that the raven is a black one: $\Pr(R)\Pr(B \mid R)$. Given we don't know the frequency of black ravens among ravens, we use our background distribution over F_i to calculate $\Pr(B \mid R) = \sum_i \Pr(B \mid F_i \wedge R)\Pr(F_i \mid R)$. In normal cases, R is admissible evidence for the frequency hypothesis F_i. So $\Pr(F_i \mid R) = \Pr(F_i)$. And $\Pr(B \mid F_i \wedge R) = i$; this is an instance of the Principal Principle (Section 2.8). Putting that all together:

$$\frac{\Pr(A \mid R \wedge B)}{\Pr(A)} = \frac{\Pr(R)}{\Pr(R)\Pr(B \mid R)} = \frac{1}{\Pr(B \mid R)} = \frac{1}{\sum_i i\Pr(F_i)}.$$

Similar reasoning gets us to this:

$$\frac{\Pr(A \mid \neg B \wedge \neg R)}{\Pr(A)} = \frac{\Pr(\neg B)}{\Pr(\neg B)\Pr(\neg R \mid \neg B)} = \frac{1}{\Pr(\neg R \mid \neg B)}.$$

But in this case, we don't need to consider chance hypotheses about the frequency of non-ravens among the non-black things, because our background evidence includes that the number of non-black things is vastly more than the number of ravens, so almost all non-black things aren't ravens: $\Pr(\neg R \mid \neg B) = 1 - \epsilon$, hence $\Pr(A \mid \neg B \wedge \neg R) \approx \Pr(A)$. So we might get a tiny improvement in the degree of support for A given a non-black, non-raven over the unaugmented background information.

The same is not true for the observation of a black raven. There the improvement of the prospects of A depends on the distribution over the chance hypotheses F_i. Suppose we have a rough model, assigning equal probability of 0.25 to each of $F_0, F_{1/3}, F_{2/3}, F_1$. Then $\sum_i i\Pr(F_i) = 0.5$, and hence $\Pr(A \mid R \wedge B)$ is significantly greater than $\Pr(A)$. (This is representative for any epistemic perspective that assigns a uniform prior to each of the hypotheses about frequency.) That is because we antecedently gave significant credence to hypotheses stating the proportion of black ravens among the ravens is low, and an encounter with a black raven was significantly in tension with those hypotheses. On the other hand, had background knowledge already indicated the proportion of black ravens was high, the confirmatory impact of the evidence would have been less.

3.6 Measuring Confirmation

Howson & Urbach (1993) summarise as follows:

> the fact that $R \wedge B$ and $\neg B \wedge \neg R$ both confirm a hypothesis does not imply that they do so with equal force. Once it is recognised that confirmation is a matter of degree, the conclusion [of Hempel's paradox] is no longer so counterintuitive, because it is compatible with $\neg B \wedge \neg R$ confirming 'All R s are B s', but to a minuscule and negligible degree. (Howson & Urbach 1993, p. 127)

Here, they suggest that part of the explanation for the judgements in the ravens paradox is a confusion between *no* confirmation and *negligible* confirmation. But their explanation invokes a notion of *degree of confirmation* that is as yet unanalysed. Degree of support of a hypothesis, relative to background evidence, there is an analysis of – that is just $\Pr(H)$. Degree of confirmation is a distinct notion, a measure of how much incremental confirmation E provides to H over the background evidence.[8]

---

[8] This is why direct comparison of degrees of support – for example, the proposal that E favours H over H' if and only if $\Pr(H \mid E) > Pr(H' \mid E)$ – is not a good measure of confirmation. Such a comparison is also about background evidence and may not represent the incremental confirmation contributed by E. Again the difference between degree of support and degree of

Howson and Urbach note that when $\Pr(H \mid E) \approx \Pr(H)$ there is a small degree of confirmation of H by E, while when $\Pr(H \mid E) \gg \Pr(H)$ there is significant degree of confirmation. These intuitions provide some fixed points to enable the construction of a measure of how much confirmation H receives from E, which is denoted by $\mathcal{C}(H, E)$. Unfortunately, there are many measures that satisfy these basic constraints – many possible hypotheses about how $\mathcal{C}(H, E)$ behaves – and yet disagree on further comparative questions of confirmation (Eells & Fitelson 2002; Fitelson 1999). I will consider one illustrative example here, the difference measure d, and relegate consideration of some other measures to the Online Appendix E.

The difference measure explains our intuitions by proposing that the degree of confirmation is the size of the difference between prior and posterior. Let us use $\mathcal{C}(H, E)$ to denote our target notion.

Difference

The difference measure is defined as $d(H, E) \overset{\text{def}}{=} \Pr(H \mid E) - \Pr(H)$.

The Difference *analysis* says that $\mathcal{C}(H, E) = d(H, E)$. (Earman 1992, p. 64; Eells & Fitelson 2002, p. 131; Jeffrey 1992, p. 72).

This measure is positive when E confirms H, zero in cases of independence, and negative in cases where E disconfirms H. Those verdicts also seem in accordance with intuition.

Suppose we adopt the Difference analysis. Let us look at how it captures the suggestion with which we began: that while a white shoe might confirm the hypothesis that all ravens are black to some extent, it won't be as much as a black raven would. The discussion in Section 3.5 gave us that $\Pr(A \mid \neg B \wedge \neg R) \gtrsim \Pr(A)$, so on the Difference measure we get immediately that $d\left(A, (\neg B \wedge \neg R)\right) \gtrsim 0$. The toy example in that same discussion gave us that $\Pr(A \mid R \wedge B) = 2\Pr(A)$, so that $d(A, R \wedge B) > \Pr(A)$. Given some non-negligible prior probability for A, this will entail that $d(A, R \wedge B) > d\left(A, (\neg B \wedge \neg R)\right)$. So if the Difference analysis is correct, we can give a successful Bayesian treatment of the intuitive difference in confirmatory power of different sorts of confirming evidence in the ravens scenario. Fitelson & Hawthorne (2010) give a full Bayesian treatment of this paradox.

How does one proceed to argue for a particular analysis of measure of confirmation, such as the Difference analysis? The typical approach is to look at particular structural constraints that we suppose confirmation ought to satisfy,

---

confirmation is pertinent. We can accept this principle however: that if $\Pr(H \mid E) > \Pr(H' \mid E)$ then the *total evidence*, including E, favours H over H'.

and check whether a proposed analysis secures those constraints. I will give a particular example. Consider this thesis:

Commutativity Non-symmetry

For some H and E, $C(H, E) \neq C(E, H)$.

Intuitively, a measure of confirmation should satisfy this (Eells & Fitelson 2002, p. 133). In the simplest case, E could be conclusive evidence for H without H being conclusive evidence for E. A coin is to be tossed twice. That it lands heads on the first toss ('First') is supportive, but inconclusive, evidence that it will land heads on both tosses ('Both'). But obviously, the evidence Both should support the hypothesis First to a higher degree.

The Difference analysis gets this right. Take the standard fair coin probability Pr, so that $\Pr(\text{First}) = 1/2$ and $\Pr(\text{Both}) = 1/4$. Because Both entails First, $\Pr(\text{First} \mid \text{Both}) = 1$, so that

$$d(\text{First}, \text{Both}) = 1 - \Pr(\text{First}) = 1/2.$$

But $\Pr(\text{Both} \mid \text{First}) = \Pr(\text{Both} \wedge \text{First})/\Pr(\text{First}) = 1/2$, so that

$$d(\text{Both}, \text{First}) = 1/2 - 1/4 = 1/4.$$

The Difference analysis successfully accommodates our intuitive verdict about Commutativity Non-Symmetry. Indeed this analysis does pretty well in accounting for a number of (non-) symmetries of C (Eells & Fitelson 2002, p. 135), though it has been subject to certain criticisms (Christensen 1999; but see Eells & Fitelson 2000). In Online Appendix E, I look at a case that poses a particular difficulty for the Difference analysis and that might be evidence for another view, the Log-Likelihood analysis (Fitelson 2007).

The debate over the Difference analysis, as over any 'conceptual analysis', rumbles on (Crupi 2021; Titelbaum 2022, pp. 225–230). There appears to be no unique best satisfier of all 'intuitive' desiderata on measures of confirmation. A pluralist attitude might suggest itself. All measures agree on the qualitative fact of *whether E* confirms H, differing only on the question *how much?* But what turns on this question? What ultimately matters for belief and action is how much the total evidence from some epistemic perspective we have adopted supports a hypothesis. Incremental confirmation matters because a confirmed theory will be more overall supported by the evidence, and the successes of the Bayesian in accounting for scientific maxims depend on that notion. But it is harder to identify scientific maxims that require a very precisely specified measure of confirmation. In most concrete cases, the existence of some plausible measure that delivers an acceptable verdict is taken as sufficient to vindicate a Bayesian approach. The plurality of measures would then reflect the plurality of our interests in quantifying confirmation; for example, sometimes we care about the absolute size of increases, in which case d is a useful measure; but sometimes we might care about relative size, in which case another measure (such as the aforementioned Log-Likelihood measure) might do better.[9] This situation isn't like the Church–Turing thesis, where radically different attempts to characterise a pre-theoretical notion of computability ended up converging on the same class of computable functions. That example is highly unrepresentative of the process of explication. Most philosophically interesting notions turn out upon precisification to splinter into finely distinguished but broadly overlapping notions, and it is hardly to be suspected that measures of incremental confirmation will be different.

3.7 Inductive Logic and Inductive Framework

The best place to finish the positive Bayesian story is where we began: with induction. Inductive inference was understood as covering all species of inference to the best explanation, including inverse inference from a sample to a population, or to a subsequent sample (Section 1.1). The synchronic aspect of this, the part that could be the subject of inductive logic, is to articulate constraints that explanation places on rational epistemic perspectives. (We emphasise the 'best explanation' part of 'inference to the best explanation'.) Induction is vindicated to the extent that a body of evidence supports the best explanation of that evidence. In Bayesian terms, broadly speaking, we accommodate induction by showing that when H explains E, that E confirms H; and that when H is the *best* explanation of E, H is probable in light of a body of total evidence including E.

One standard view of explanation is that an explanation shows how an otherwise puzzling event is to be accommodated and made comprehensible within a broader framework. Van Fraassen (1980, chapter 6) suggests that explanations are proffered as answers to 'why'-questions; to explain an event is to provide relevant information about an event and its participants, relative to the background presuppositions of the questioner. Very often, though perhaps not invariably, this will take the form of 'information about its causal history' (Lewis 1986b, p. 217). So to explain why the vase broke could involve citing a cause of the vase breaking, such as its being dropped. Yet a question coming from a different background might demand a different answer. Suppose our

---

[9] Some have argued against d on these grounds (Schlesinger 1995; Zalabardo 2009), because a large increase in relative risk (e.g., a thousand-fold increase in cancer risk after radiation exposure) might be associated with a very low value of d(cancer, radiation). It is actually by no means clear that the pre-theoretical judgements about confirmation we are attempting to systematise are at variance with this result.

request for explanation takes this form: 'Yes, I know it was dropped, but why did it *break*?'); in that case, the request for explanation might be satisfied by providing information about the fragility of the vase. This is still information about the causal history.

Very often, causal relations are manifest in relations of statistical dependence. When C is a body of information about causes, and E some effect of those causes, very often $\Pr(E \mid C) > \Pr(E)$.[10] The broken vase is more probable given it was dropped than otherwise. The background is involved in selecting a pertinent probability function: it is more probable that the vase breaks given it was fragile and dropped, than that it is dropped alone, given a background that does not build in the fragility of the vase. Putting this together: very often, to explain an event is to offer information, relative to a background body of evidence, such that the likelihood of the event given the information is greater than its prior probability:

> where the hypotheses are specific, a hypothesis, H, explains the data better than H', if true, just when H would make the data more expected than H'. In judging which hypothesis renders the data most understandable, we consider nothing more than which hypothesis renders it most expected. (Henderson 2014, p. 700)

A theory is explanatory to the extent that it encapsulates such information, so that – very often – H explains E just when it renders E more likely than otherwise, $\Pr(E \mid H) > \Pr(E)$. An elementary application of Bayes' theorem then entails:

Bayesian Explanation

When H explains E by making it more likely than otherwise, relative to some background evidence and conception of evidential relevance, then E confirms H: if $\Pr(E \mid H) > \Pr(E)$, then $\Pr(H \mid E) > \Pr(H)$.

Recall an example from Section 1.1. The Channelled Scablands of western Washington state is a complex landscape of braided channels, exhibiting the characteristics seen in microcosm in dry gorges incised into harder rock, characteristics such as potholes, gravel bars, and scoured deep grooves. Bretz hypothesised that this landscape was indeed the effect of a cataclysmic flood, in which debris-laden water was discharged on such a vast scale that an existing dissected plateau was filled beyond the capacity of its existing drainage, so that water spilled over the top of the plateau, removed the existing topsoil, and carved branching and reuniting channels into the bedrock (Baker 2009, pp. 402–403).

---

[10] Causation is not quite perfectly manifest in statistical dependence, since there may be causes that do not raise the probability of their effects (Glynn 2010, pp. 349–353; Rosen 1978).

The hypothesis certainly makes the evidence more probable than otherwise: given attested geological mechanisms as the background assumptions, a gigantic flood would produce just what is seen at the landscape scale.

Nevertheless, Bretz' hypothesis took many years to gain acceptance, despite its explanatory merits, because the source of such an extraordinary volume of water was unknown. Subsequent evidence of an ice sheet intruding into Idaho suggested the existence of a lake formed behind an ice dam, containing 2,100 km^3 of water and covering much of western Montana. The collapse of the ice dam, it is hypothesised, would have resulted in the evacuation of the whole of this body of water in a mere 48 hours. It was only after the background evidence provided a remotely plausible source for the required water (with the required erosive power) that Bretz' hypothesis was adopted. So part of what made it ultimately the best explanation was not only its explanation of the data, but its prior plausibility. As before, likelihoods alone do not suffice. To generalise:

Bayesian IBE

H is the best explanation of the data E when (i) H explains E, $\Pr(E \mid H) > \Pr(E)$, and (ii) H is most probable among competing explanations.

Bayesian inference to the best explanation also shows the limits of IBE. For it is quite possible for H to be the best explanation of E and for some rival to be far more credible, antecedently. A theory may exhibit many explanatory virtues, such as simplicity, elegance, and deployment of familiar mechanisms that enable it to generate understanding, and so on – all those features contributing to a theory's 'loveliness' (Lipton 2004, p. 59) – and yet not be probable: 'explanatory goodness, whatever it is, looks to be at least somewhat independent of prior conditional [probability]' (Weisberg 2009, p. 130). Moreover, it may be quite rational to have attitudes that mirror this perspective. In the absence of information favouring the enormous glacial lake, most geologists were sure that (i) Bretz' catastrophic flood hypothesis was an excellent explanation of the data, and (ii) that less unified, ragged, and unfamiliar hypotheses were to be preferred.

What we want, of course, is a story that explains the rationality of both parties. Bretz was open to the existence of a gigantic flood, compelled by the field evidence that seemed to demand it. For him, we may suppose, what was vivid is just how low $\Pr(E \mid \neg H)$ was, which ensured that relative to his background evidence, $\Pr(H \mid E)$ was sufficiently high for overall credibility. The rival view involved a different perspective, $\Pr'$, such that $\Pr'(H)$ was so low that $\Pr'(H \mid E)$ could still not suffice for credibility. This difference in background perspective might accommodate the joint rationality of everyone involved at the earlier stages, though perhaps even $\Pr'(H \mid E \wedge L)$ should be high, where L is the evidence favouring the glacial lake. If 'inference to the best explanation' is understood to involve inference based on explanatory considerations divorced from prior credibility and background knowledge, then it is lucky that Bayesians cannot reconstruct IBE in that sense.[11] But very often, explanatory factors are correlated with the likelihoods of evidence given hypotheses (Henderson 2014, p. 709), and thus the Bayesian offers an explication of the merits of IBE, when it has merit.

The Bayesian reconstruction of inference to the best explanation is a key part of the Bayesian account of induction, alongside the more particular maxims of inductive methodology discussed earlier (Sections 3.1, 3.3–3.5). The role of background assumptions has been a constant refrain. And this is just as it should be. The upshot of the earlier discussion of Hume's problem of induction in Section 1.6 was that a theory of the relation '*E* supports *H* relative to standards *S*' is needed – and I have offered a broadly Bayesian account of this notion.

This point can be sharpened. Let's consider a highly abstracted but quite general representation of 'classic' inductive inferences. A possible world is an infinite binary sequence of outcomes (like the results of successive coin tosses); the correct theory of a given world is simply identified with the theory that predicts each outcome (it needn't have more 'abstract' theoretical structure); hence the space of possibilities is given by the set of all such sequences. A broadly Bayesian theory of inductive evidential support assigns probabilities to hypotheses based on initial subsequences; it is a classic case of inverse inference from a sample to a population. Some Bayesian results can be established that seem to vindicate induction. Suppose H_i is the sequence that hypothesis H predicts for the initial i outcomes. Thus $H = H_\infty$, and for each i, $H \vDash H_i$. It can be shown that, so long as $\Pr(H) > 0$,

$$\lim_{i \to \infty} \Pr(H_{i+1} \mid H_i) = 1.$$

That is, the probability of the correct hypothesis tends to 1 as more outcomes conformable with it accumulate (Howson 2000, p. 72). This looks like a substantive vindication of ampliative inference.

The first limitation to note is that the requirement that $\Pr(H) > 0$, which may look innocuous, is extremely substantive. This space of hypotheses is the Cantor space, the set of all infinite binary sequences; that space is uncountable. If each

---

[11] Van Fraassen offers another Bayesian argument against IBE (1989, p. 166), construed as an inference that boosts the posterior credibility of explanatory hypotheses over and above the extent to which the evidence favours them; so-construed, what I've been discussing is not IBE, and luckily so, since the rule van Fraassen is discussing seems manifestly irrational if truth is what is sought.

hypothesis were given equal probability, as under the standard Lebesgue measure, each hypothesis would have prior probability zero, and the result would apply to none of them. If some hypothesis is eventually to be maximally supported by the total evidence, it must be assigned some initial positive probability – indeed, there must be at most countably many hypotheses assigned positive probability. So almost all possible hypotheses about the sequence of outcomes need to be excluded *ab initio*. Of course, one might be unlucky enough to assign probability 0 to the true hypothesis, in which case after finitely many data points all the live hypotheses will have been refuted. At that point, one must simply restart with a new hypotheses space, the set of all infinite binary sequences which begin with the previously observed data. That is still an uncountable space (it simply involves pre-pending the observed data to each element of the Cantor space), and subject to the same worries. So the choice of epistemic perspective already has to make substantive assumptions about which possible hypotheses to consider 'live'; assumptions which are required before confirmation can occur, and even in the presence of observed data, are not fixed by that data.

Secondly, the result tells us nothing about the speed of convergence. Eventually, every rival hypotheses is eliminated by some data point. But after any finite time, the data points eliminating incorrect hypotheses may be arbitrarily far away. So to ensure robust inductive support of the correct hypothesis, we shall have to make the further substantive assumption that the data we have so far are a *representative sample* of the whole population. That assumption seems *a priori* quite strong; an infinite population in which after a certain point no F s are G can nevertheless begin with arbitrarily many initial F s which are G s; hypotheses of that sort simply have to be excluded by fiat. Indeed, whatever we do, we shall need to make some assumptions about what sort of overall hypotheses are supported by a given initial sequence of the data. For example, how quickly should we 'learn from experience'? How many consecutive initial 1s should it take for us to become more confident than not that all the outcomes will be 1s? How inclined we are to judge that the temporally initial conditions might well be *un*representative of the whole sequence of outcomes? For example, were we to note that in the actual world, the early universe is very unlike the universe over most of the time, we might be hesitant to draw any conclusions from the early data – that naturally requires some judgement about when the data stops being early.[12]

---

[12] Compare also hypotheses about pandemic spread: we should expect those who get the disease early to be systematically different from more cautious individuals who delay infection, in a way that cannot be judged without assumptions about the relative proportions of these individuals in the population.

These kinds of assumptions are most readily understood as constraints on conditional probabilities: what distribution over hypotheses does a given piece of evidence license? These examples show that the Bayesian not only invokes prior probabilities, but may well invoke conditional probabilities too that need not be uniquely constrained.

Any actionable inductive practice must unavoidably involve some prior assumptions; a third relatum of the evidential support relation, an epistemic perspective encoding both antecedent judgements of hypothesis plausibility *and* prior conditional judgements of evidential relevance. A virtue of the Bayesian account I've developed is that it makes these assumptions explicit in the evidential probability model of epistemic perspectives.

A challenge sometimes posed is that this explicit invocation of a probability model shows that I haven't really offered a theory of evidential support after all – that this is only an 'inductive framework', rather than an 'inductive logic' that guides scientific argument:

> particular inferences can almost always be brought into accord with the Bayesian scheme by assigning degrees of belief more or less *ad hoc*, but we learn nothing from this agreement. What we want is an explanation of scientific argument; what the Bayesians give us is a theory of learning, indeed a theory of personal learning. But arguments are more or Jess impersonal; I make an argument to persuade anyone informed of the premises, and in doing so I am not reporting any bit of autobiography. .... Alternatively, and more hopefully, Bayesians may suggest that we give arguments exactly because there are general principles restricting belief, principles that are widely subscribed to, and in giving arguments we are attempting to show that, supposing our audience has certain beliefs, they must in view of these principles have other beliefs, those we are trying to establish. There is nothing controversial about this suggestion, and I endorse it. What is controversial is that the general principles required for argument can best be understood as conditions restricting prior probabilities in a Bayesian framework. Sometimes they can, perhaps, but I think that when arguments turn on relating evidence to theory, it is very difficult to explicate them in a plausible way within the Bayesian framework. (Glymour 1981, pp. 74–5; see also Strevens 2004)

The first point to make in response is that this objection seems to require too much of *logic*, regardless of induction. The second is that only some Bayesians offer theories of personal learning; not this one. The final point is to note that the proof of Bayesian principles is in the pudding; a review of the cases discussed previously, in which Bayesian precepts rationalise and systematise scientific conceptions of good evidence, provides defeasible grounds favouring the Bayesian model.

4 Uniqueness and the Problem of the Priors

I begin this section by outlining various issues around the justification of prior probabilities, and frame responses as permissivist or impermissivist (Section 4.1). In Section 4.2, I describe some permissivist attempts to explain away the demand for unique rational priors. In Section 4.3, I look at the Principle of Indifference and its role in attempts at constructing a unique prior, and describe the charge of inconsistency levelled at it. I turn to formal approaches to constructing prior probabilities at the end of the section: to Carnap's inductive logic in Section 4.4, and Solomonoff's algorithmic probability approach in the concluding Section 4.5. Neither ultimately fares well.

4.1 The Problem of the Priors

The 'problem of the priors' is not one problem, but rather a cluster of issues that circle around the plurality of coherent evidential probability functions.

1. One issue concerns belief and action: if there are many epistemic perspectives, but we need to plump for a particular credence function to feed into our deliberations, how ought we choose an epistemic perspective to adopt? This issue was introduced in Section 2.8, but any solution will depend on what we say in this section.

2. A second issue concerns the *rationality* of epistemic perspectives. We might want to say that conspiracy theorists, cranks, and those who persist in salvaging a preferred hypotheses by denial of auxiliary assumptions are being *unreasonable*, even if, technically, they seem to accurately deploy scientific standards. The source of such recalcitrance, on the Bayesian view, lies in the prior distribution over hypotheses. If epistemic perspectives provide ideals for rational belief, the space of epistemic perspectives must be more tightly constrained than hitherto.

3. A related issue concerns *procedural* rationality. The vindication in Section 3 of induction, or of the canons of scientific methodology, required assumptions about the priors. Other priors would vindicate different methodological maxims: counter-induction, preferences for unrepresentative samples and biased evidence. But it would be unreasonable to use these alternative maxims; a reasonable person wouldn't respond to evidence in the ways these perspectives appear to license. The Bayesian picture accommodates rational responses to evidence, but seems unduly tolerant of other responses, to the extent where scientists 'may disagree on sufficiently many important questions that the consensus required for scientific progress is undermined' (Strevens 2006, p. 82).

4. A further issue concerns the *objectivity* of science. Science is a self-regulating community, with broad intersubjective agreement on procedures and on the space of legitimate theorising. 'One's expectation, or hope if you will, is that the explanation of the intersubjective agreement on such matters is not merely historical or sociological but has a justificatory character' (Earman 1992, pp. 137–138). Without robust internal constraints on the allowable epistemic perspectives, scientific consensus looks more like the product of exclusion than the ineluctable workings of the scientific method.

5. The Bayesian picture seems to put the cart before the horse. It puts attitudes, whether actual or idealised, in the position that should rightly be occupied by the evidential connections that justify those attitudes: 'our judgment of the relevance of evidence to theory depends on the perception of a structural connection between the two ... degree of belief is, at best, epiphenomenal' (Glymour 1981, pp. 92–93).

6. Evidential probabilities must represent ignorance, to be sufficiently amenable to updating in light of new evidence: 'our initial beliefs should not unfairly favor one empirical hypothesis over another. ... an adequate account of how to respond to evidence should be neutral and "let the data speak for itself"' (Meacham 2014, pp. 1193–1194). But Bayesian priors 'exercise a controlling influence' over subsequent attitudes, and are insufficiently neutral (Norton 2011, pp. 428–429).

There are many ideas swirling around here, and they are not all pulling in the same direction. A central tension is whether the priors should be neutral, open to being guided by evidence, or instead impose rigid confines on the acceptable responses to evidence. To ensure the rationality and objectivity of inductive practice, we want to require epistemic perspectives to exhibit a uniformity of response to a given piece of information, at least if they share their other background information. That desired uniformity of response across perspectives mandates a non-uniform response to hypotheses by those perspectives, because some hypotheses will gain significant support from the evidence they predict only if 'unreasonable' responses to evidence are deployed. There is nothing incoherent about the theory Hume entertains, that while bread so far has given us nourishment and support, from now on it will not. But in a scenario where it is true, belief in it on the basis of the evidence can only come from a quite different theory of evidential support than the one we actually utilise. This is perhaps another manifestation of the phenomenon of the underdetermination of theory by evidence.

The problem of the priors, as I see it, is to resolve this tension between treating theories fairly, not letting prejudice scupper their chances at confirmation, and responding to evidence in a productive way that eventually leads to reasonable scientific consensus. Two approaches suggest themselves. The *permissive* response acknowledges that there are many acceptable responses to a given body of total evidence, and no guarantee that the true hypotheses will be eventually favoured by the evidence regardless of which possible epistemic standards are considered (Section 2.8). Each standard favours some theories over others, but no one standard is singled out prior to experience, hence no theories are disqualified *ab initio*. To secure scientific progress, the permissivist allows (i) it is rational to opt for one epistemic perspective over another, even holding fixed total evidence, and even without its approach being favoured by some decisive epistemic reason; and (ii) shared situational and sociological factors encourage different scientists to opt for more or less similar perspectives. These two factors explain both the wide-spread agreement on evidential standards, and the rationality of those standards; the drawback many see is that the convergence on common standards isn't explained by their being rationally required, which seems to leave the approach open to a charge of arbitrariness.

The *impermissive* response is different. Impermissivists deny that there are alternative equally good ways of responding to evidence. I will focus on the species of impermissivist who asserts that there is a unique acceptable epistemic perspective for any given body of total evidence. Such an impermissivist accepts:

Uniqueness
'There is a unique rational response to any particular body of evidence' (Kopec & Titelbaum 2016, p. 189); for any 'evidential situation . . . there is a uniquely rational state to be in right then' (Greco & Hedden 2016, p. 392).

Given Uniqueness and the discussion in Section 3.7, it will turn out that many hypotheses are guaranteed not to be supported by the evidence, having been excluded from the start by the unique epistemic perspective compatible with null evidence (Meacham 2014, p. 1213). So not every hypothesis is treated fairly, and (depending on the interaction of Uniqueness with modality) it could turn out that in some scenarios the truth cannot be rationally supported by the evidence. The defenders of Uniqueness are sensitive to this concern, and the concrete imple-mentations of Uniqueness that have been put forward, and that I will discuss, all attempt to build in neutrality between possible hypotheses as a desideratum. The objectivity and rationality of science is secured, as a more than sociological matter, so long as the scientific method follows the dictates of the uniquely rational epistemic perspective – but again, defenders of Uniqueness have used conformity with standard scientific maxims as constraints on the construction of the unique function. Uniqueness may hold out the promise of resolving the problems of the priors.

The principal problems for Uniqueness are two:[13] the manifest implausibility of denying that there can ever be reasonable disagreements about the significance of a piece of evidence (Rosen 2001, p. 71); and the challenge of constructing or defining the uniquely rational epistemic perspective. Some defenders of Uniqueness have wanted to dodge the second challenge, suggesting that while there is a uniquely rational perspective to take, given any body of evidence, it is not in general easily known to us (White 2009, section 3). Whether that is viable or not, everyone can agree that the actual provision of a uniquely rational prior would show permissivism to be false, so I will concentrate on constructive proposals in what follows. Proponents of particular constructive projects are known as *objective Bayesians*, and so I will focus on the rivalry between Bayesian permissivists and extant objective Bayesians in what follows. I wish to resist the appropriation of the terminology of 'objective Bayesianism' by proponents of Uniqueness however; the permissivist theory of epistemic perspectives defended in Section 2 is not a subjectivist account, but it is compatible with permissivism. I make no secret below of the fact that I have a great deal of sympathy for the project of permissivist objective Bayesianism.

4.2 Permissivism and Priors

One popular early broadly permissivist approach was to try and argue that while permissivism was true of 'informationless' priors, all such priors end up converging to a Unique shared conditional probability when given the same evidence – the priors *wash out*, as it is sometimes put: 'empirical evidence will bring together any two points of view provided they are not dogmatic with respect to each other' (Gaifman & Snir 1982, p. 498). The mathematical elegance of these convergence-of-opinion theorems is undeniable, but they have strong assumptions and rather weak conclusions (Earman 1992, pp. 141–154). The requirement that the perspectives to be merged not be dogmatic with respect to each other requires that they assign probability zero to the same

---

[13] Permissivism and impermissivism, in my usage, are theses about epistemic perspectives, not individual attitudes. Kopec & Titelbaum (2016, pp. 190–192) note that 'Uniqueness' has been used to label many different claims. This creates an opportunity to deflect certain challenges. For example, perhaps the uniqueness of ideal rationality is compatible with permissivism about individual credence – maybe you can be rational if your credence suitably approximates the ideal, subject to your cognitive limitations. Perhaps permissiveness about evidential standards is practically inert, because individual rationality requires deference to peers in a way that secures credal agreement.

outcomes. In the absence of Regularity, and in the presence of very rich spaces of possible hypotheses, very many pairs of acceptable perspectives will therefore not meet the preconditions to be reconcilable with one another. The convergence results also give no indication of the time frame for the priors to wash out, rendering them ineffective as an explanation of current scientific consensus on evidential support.

Recalling that evidential support and confirmation have been defined relative to an epistemic perspective (evidential probability model), the permissivist can argue that rationality and objectivity have been secured. It is an objective fact that $Pr(H \mid E) > Pr'(H \mid E)$, for suitable Pr and Pr'; that is the kind of fact that inductive logic yields. The choice as to whether Pr and Pr' ought to feature in scientific *inference* is a matter that goes beyond inductive logic.

> One might respond at this point by asking, Where do the probability models M come from? and how does one choose an 'appropriate' probability model in a given inductive logical context? These are good questions. However, it is not clear that they must be answered by the inductive logician *qua* logician. . . . It is not the business of the inductive logician to tell people which probability models they should use (presumably, that is an epistemic or pragmatic question), but once a probability model is specified, the inductive logical relations in that model . . . are determined objectively and non-contingently. In the present approach, the duty of the inductive logician is (simply) to explicate the [confirmation]-function—not to decide which probability models should be used in which contexts. (Fitelson 2005, pp. 391–392; cf. Earman 1992, p. 159)

One might follow the discussion of Section 3.2 and appeal to context as supplying evidential standards, just as it supplies other parameters to complete overtly unsaturated expressions. It has been argued that natural language quantifier phrases like 'every person' and 'some plant' must involve reference to domains of quantification, supplied automatically by context when no overt domain is specified (Stanley 2000; Stanley & Szabó 2000). While epistemic contextualism about 'knows' is fiercely contested, that 'is confirmed' or 'is supported' are gradable adjectives is quite plausible. On the present view natural language uses of 'supports' or 'confirms' will pick up some contextually supplied probability model in order to have a semantic content at all; it is unsurprising that in the course of a single conversation the same model will be supplied for all occurrences of 'E confirms H' where no epistemic perspective is explicitly mentioned. The contextualist approach needn't require that any explicit calculation take place to generate an appropriate probability model; it will be one that 'fits' the general background beliefs of speakers and makes the claims they make about confirmation and evidence broadly true. (Again accommodation will play a role here: say '*E* supports *H*' and you thereby make your context one in which the relevant standards make that true, other things being equal.)

Invoking context may seem to have all the advantages of theft over honest toil. So the permissivist may wish to be more specific about why some epistemic perspective might be a candidate for contextual selection. Permissivists have a story to tell about this. It will be one that, like Hume's own account of induction, aims to explain where it cannot justify. There is no pre-given ideal to which we must conform; the explanation of our shared epistemic standards then must appeal to factors that might plausibly produce the phenomenon.

Hume appealed to both 'custom or habit'(1999/1748, para. 5.5) and 'instinct' (1999/1748, para. 9.6), and doubtless both, in updated forms, may play a role in explaining our inductive practice. (Nowadays we might well explain instinct in its turn as the product of natural selection.) The inclination towards having certain priors that produce relatively swift 'learning from experience' (or perhaps, 'jumping to inductive conclusions') is certainly evident in practice. The rational critique of such priors will generally proceed not from selecting some other prior *a priori*, but selecting some rival prior, more cautious or responsible, that resembles the hasty prior in many ways. (Perhaps it will be one that takes the same evidence to be confirmatory of the same hypotheses, but where the degree of confirmation is lower, and hence any approach to inductively-based confidence in a generalisation will be slower.) The point is that the scientific method might involve a refinement of our habits, not the heroic creation of a theory of evidential support out of whole cloth.

Another factor must be sociological – Hume's 'custom'. Scientists are trained, not born. They are enculturated into the scientific mindset, learning through exposure to their mentors and the literature which hypotheses are seen as viable, what sort of evidence is taken to provide a compelling test, and so on. If the scientific method can be captured by some constraints on epistemic perspectives, and those constraints are widely endorsed, and there is considerable benefit to being in line with community opinion on confirmation (as there is in actual scientific communities), that is a prudential reason for budding scientists to respect those constraints in the evaluation of evidence.

The permissivist who appeals to sociological or instinctual factors does open themselves up to a charge of arbitrariness (Feldman 2007, pp. 204–205; White 2005, pp. 451–452). Had the background factors been different – had you been differently trained – different epistemic perspective would have been open to you to adopt. While your current standards suggest that *E* is evidence for *H*, other standards you could easily have had (had you gone to graduate school elsewhere and had a different mentor) would suggest that *E* undermines *H*. Suppose you chose your graduate school for epistemically irrelevant reasons.

(Perhaps, like me, you wanted to be close to New York City.) Can you really think your current attitudes about evidential support are defensible given their fragility?

But the counterfactual about evidential support in no way suggests that you have to dissociate yourself from your current standards once you acknowledge permissivism. What it is to adopt some standards as your own is to regard them as conducing to rational belief. If your response to cases is to be open to thinking those standards might not be reliable, then one hasn't fully adopted those standards. Once one has adopted them, however, one is committed *ex cathedra* to judging that other standards are defective. After all, while H is likely to be true given E, those other standards say it is likely to be false! So those standards will probably get things wrong. One might, as a permissivist, think that one is *lucky* to have been trained in such a way as to have reliable standards, unlike one's peers elsewhere, who are rational but unlucky. But one cannot take their rationality to be a reason to abandon reliable standards, either by suspending judgement on the verdicts of one's own standards, or plumping for rival standards. There is no standpoint-independent 'meta-perspective' that gives one neutral standards for evaluating epistemic standards (Schoenfield 2012, p. 202; cf. Horowitz 2014, pp. 42–45); there is only where you are.[14]

Whatever the merits of this response to the worry about arbitrariness, it remains unsettling to think that scientific rationality could involve any element of luck or convention. And a compelling answer to any sort of permissivism would be the provision of a rational prior that supported our inductive practice while meeting the desiderata of neutrality and non-arbitrariness implicit in the problem of the priors. In the remainder of this section, I will consider a number of attempts to carry out this task.

4.3 Constructing Priors: the Principle of Indifference

All prominent attempts to construct neutral priors take as their starting point the Leibnizian idea that probability is graded possibility. The uniquely best measure of the degree of possibility – the best probability function – is the one that reflects the natural structure of the space of possibilities. Various proposals have been offered that claim to discern this natural structure. The *classical theory* of probability is a good place to start.

> The theory of chance consists in reducing all the events of the same kind to a certain number of cases equally possible, that is to say, to such as we may be

---

[14] Similar things might be said about other standards – perhaps the right thing to say about aesthetic standards is broadly permissivist, but acknowledging that others can be rational in deploying different aesthetic standards doesn't require you to change your evaluation of artwork.

equally undecided about in regard to their existence, and in determining the number of cases favorable to the event whose probability is sought. The ratio of this number to that of all the cases possible is the measure of this probability, which is thus simply a fraction whose numerator is the number of favorable cases and whose denominator is the number of all the cases possible. (Laplace 1995/1825, pp. 6–7)

The classical theory says that 'equal possibilities' should be assigned equal probabilities, and that every probability is reducible to some combination of equal probabilities. The theory was presented as an account of physical probability. It was inadequate to that task, as it could not handle infinite outcome spaces, and excluded the possibility of basic cases with unequal probabilities, such as a biased die.[15] But it is more promising as an account of prior probability. Laplace talks of cases about which 'we *may* be equally undecided about in regard to their existence' (my emphasis), and this can be read as suggesting a lack of evidence either way. In that case, Laplace is offering an early version of the:

Principle of Indifference (POI)

'if there is no *known* reason for predicating of our subject one rather than another of several alternatives, then relatively to such knowledge the assertions of each of these alternatives have an *equal* probability' (Keynes 1921, p. 42; cf. White 2009, sections 1–2).

The POI is more modest than the classical theory because it doesn't purport to assign probabilities to all outcomes. It is also a principle that takes an explicitly epistemic attitude, of indifference between possibilities and yields a determinate probability distribution. The POI, as constructed, is designed to ensure the neutrality of initial probabilities over hypotheses. It works well in many toy examples. What is the rational probability that a goat is behind a given door of the three before you, if two of them have a goat? You have no reason to suppose a goat is behind any particular door; you shouldn't be more confident for no reason, so you should be as neutral as possible, assigning 2/3 probability to each proposition of the form 'a goat is behind door *n*'. This is an implementation of Uniqueness, because POI says the uniquely rational perspective in a situation of equipollence is the indifferent one.

From the perspective of inductive logic, this enforcement of neutrality makes other problems of the priors worse. For the indifferent prior distribution seems to make very poor predictions about inductive support. A binary A/B process of unknown bias will occur 9 times (Weisberg 2011, p. 507).

---

[15] Or, if '▢', '▢', and so on, are not basic cases in the case of a weighted die, then what are the basic cases that allow, for example, a 1/5 chance of getting a '▢'?

You have no reason to think it fair; nor to think it biased; nor, if biased, that the bias is in any specific direction. The POI mandates, it seems,[16] a uniform distribution over each hypothesis, that is, over all 2^9 possible outcome sequences. What is the conditional probability that all outcomes are Bs, given the first 8 are Bs?

$$\Pr(9\ \text{Bs} \mid 8\ \text{Bs}) = \frac{\Pr(\text{BBBBBBBBB})}{\Pr(\text{BBBBBBBBB} \vee \text{BBBBBBBBA})} = \frac{1/2^9}{2/2^9} = \frac{1}{2}.$$

The POI has generated not just uniformity over hypotheses about outcomes prior to experience, but also posterior to experience. Given a process of previously unknown bias, inductive plausibility strongly suggests that 8 (or 88, or 888, ...) consecutive Bs is strong support for a particular hypothesis about bias. We should at least be able to adopt priors that *permit* us to ignore anti-inductive hypotheses, such as regarding BBBBBBBBA as less plausible than BBBBBBBBB. But indifference mandates that we give undue regard to such hypotheses. Neutrality trumps inductive plausibility.

Some might challenge this. In a process of unknown bias, we ought to be indifferent not over individual sequences, but over the *frequencies* those sequences exhibit. Then we should be indifferent over the space of hypotheses '9 As', '8 As, 1 B', ... , '9 Bs'. I will return to the merits of this particular proposal in Section 4.4, but there is a worry before we even work out the details: what mandates our representing the problem this way, rather than the first way? This brings out the fact that every application of the POI involves – just as the classical theory does – a classification of the space of all possibilities into 'basic cases' or 'alternatives' between which we are indifferent. We have to do this; there are so many possible worlds that the only indifference measure over them assigns every possibility no probability at all. So we have to partition the space of possible worlds into basic alternatives in order to get a non-trivial indifference measure. But there are different ways of carving up the very same possibilities (Meacham 2014, pp. 1193–1198). Consider this example.

Mystery Cube (van Fraassen 1989, p. 303)

A tool factory produces metal cubes with edge length x, where x lies in the interval $[1, 3]$ (i.e., $1 \leq x \leq 3$). What is the probability that a cube has edge length ≥ 2 cm, given that it was produced by that factory?

---

[16] Keynes (1921, chapter 4) suggests that in a case of unknown bias like this, ideal rationality forbids any numerical assignment of probability; that saves the POI at the cost of drastically reducing its concrete role in fixing the priors.

Table 3 Applying the POI to different partitions
of Mystery Cube.

Possible cases	Favourable-to-*L*	$\Pr(L)$
edge length $\in$ $[1, 3]$	length $\in$ $[2, 3]$	$1/2$
face area $\in$ $[1, 9]$	area $\in$ $[4, 9]$	$5/8$
cube volume $\in$ $[1, 27]$	volume $\in$ $[8, 27]$	$19/26$

The issue is that there are logically equivalent ways of dividing up the same possibilities which seem to give different answers. For we could also represent the possible outputs of the cube factory in terms of their face area, or their volume. Let L be the proposition 'a cube has side length ≥ 2'. The possible cases, and favourable-to-L cases, are detailed in Table 3.

Apply the POI naively, and we get inconsistent probability assignments. Hesitate to apply it, on the grounds that different partitions give rise to different judgements of epistemic symmetry (White 2009, section 3), and we get no probability assignment at all, even though the POI 'is supposed to fill the gap left by missing information' (van Fraassen 1989, p. 304).

One might have the sense that the POI has been applied incorrectly. In the mystery cube case, we have a problem with multiple representations. Given a representation, for example, that areas were between 1 and 9 cm^2, POI was applied to the $[1, 9]$ interval to generate the probabilities. But this is manifestly implausible, since it applies indifference to features of the representation, rather than features of the problem represented. A better model would be to identify which representations are merely 'modes of presentation' of the original problem, using those to define a class of transformations that preserve the structure of the original problem. As Rosenkrantz puts it:

> The needed invariances, however, are not obtained by looking at parameter transformations *per se*, but at transformations of the problem itself into equivalent form. Given the statement of the problem, it may for example, be indifferent in what scale units the data are expressed. Such 'indifference between problems' determines what parameter transformations are admissible – not the other way around. (Rosenkrantz 1977, p. 63; see also Jaynes 1968, p. 128)

Then POI must be applied in a way that is invariant under those transformations; in practice, to some measure over $[1, 3]$ cm that is equivalent to $[1, 9]$ cm^2. In the mystery cube case, the allowable transformations are dilations, so the right measure μ on the intervals is $\mu[x, y] = \log y - \log x$. Then we get the 'right' answer (van Fraassen 1989, p. 310):[17]

$$\Pr(L) = \frac{\mu[2,3]}{\mu[1,3]} = \frac{\log 3 - \log 2}{\log 3 - \log 1} = \frac{2\log 3 - 2\log 2}{2\log 3 - 2\log 1} = \frac{\log 9 - \log 4}{\log 9 - \log 1} = \frac{\mu[4,9]}{\mu[1,9]}.$$

This kind of move requires some substantive knowledge about which formal transformations of descriptions of the space of possibilities are those that preserve the 'essential' symmetries of the problem. So this cannot be a purely neutral ignorance prior. Once we have recognised that most circumstances in which we'd wish to apply POI actually involve some background knowledge, the POI turns out to be inapplicable. But there is a generalisation of the POI that might apply:

Uniqueness (Maximum Entropy)

Given a set $\mathbb{C}$ of probability functions meeting certain constraints imposed by the evidence, the uniquely determined evidential probability in light of that evidence is the $\Pr \in \mathbb{C}$ such that $H(\Pr) = -\sum_{\omega} \Pr(\omega) \log \Pr(\omega)$ is maximised, assuming there is exactly one (Jaynes 1957).

The rationale for the Maximum Entropy principle is that entropy is a measure of uninformativeness; so maximum entropy subject to constraints is a way of maximising neutrality given those constraints (Seidenfeld 1986; Williamson 2011, section 8). The Maximum Entropy approach does hold out the prospect, unlike the original POI, of both satisfying our desire for neutrality and our desire to have probability functions that are responsive to potential experience (Williamson 2011, section 9).

Unfortunately, it would be too hasty to think this gives us a case for Uniqueness. Whenever the uniform distribution is consistent with the background evidence, it always has maximum entropy. But there is no guarantee, if the constraints rule out the uniform distribution, that there is a unique entropy maximising distribution (Shackel & Rowbottom 2020); maximum entropy may turn out to be a moderate permissivist view. This non-uniqueness, as in the original problem cases for the POI, turns out to depend on how the problem scenario is represented. (In Williamson's (2011, section 10) approach, this is manifest in an explicit language-relativity – see also Weisberg 2011, p. 508.)

Ultimately, the POI and Maximum Entropy proposals are plausible because they answer, if we are lucky, the twin demands of Uniqueness and neutrality. But once permissivism is brought into view, a view that generates unique

---

[17] Even this fails for some cases where there is no neat class of allowable transformations, for example, those involving both translation and dilation (Milne 1983).

probability distributions doesn't look neutral. For example, the original POI mandated a policy of taking any new evidence to be irrelevant to confirmation; while this may be a permissible attitude, it hardly looks mandatory. The most natural maximum entropy distribution that permits responsiveness to experience is one that determines a very specific rule about *how responsive* to be (Weisberg 2011, p. 508) – yet, intuitively, there is room for variation in appetites for epistemic risk, from Jamesian boldness to Cliffordian timidity. Enforced neutrality between hypotheses leads to overly determinate prescriptions about responsiveness to evidence. (In the Bayesian framework, the fact that unconditional probabilities of hypotheses are expectations of conditional probabilities given possible evidence – that is, policies for responding to evidence – yokes these two quantities together.) If instead we are not prescriptive about $\Pr(H \mid E)$, remaining neutral to the extent we can over its value, then we won't be as interested in prescriptivism about $\Pr(H)$, and we can secure indifference, where appropriate, by substantive assumptions about the problem scenario at hand. These observations apply also to the remaining attempts to construct explicit unique priors I will consider.

4.4 Constructing Priors: Carnap's Inductive Logic

Treating Carnap at this point is anachronistic; his contributions to inductive logic really kicked off the field, along with Hempel's, and everyone working on the topic since is indebted to their framing. But Carnap offered a particular recipe for constructing unique priors, one that would – if successful – vindicate the idea of an inductive logic. For just as deductive logic gives us relations on sentences in virtue of logical form, so Carnap proposed to give a purely formal account of evidential support:

> While a statement of statistical probability asserts a matter of fact, a statement of inductive probability is of a purely logical nature. If hypothesis and evidence are given, the probability can be determined by logical analysis and mathematical calculation. (Carnap 1955, p. 3)

Given the preceding discussion, it seems the prospects for such a proposal are fairly dim, but it is nevertheless worth going through the details, for completeness' sake and because it allows us to bolster some earlier conclusions against purely formal treatments of epistemic support (Section 1.5). It also feeds nicely into the upcoming treatment of algorithmic probability (Section 4.5) and allows us to touch on some issues, like 'gruesome' predicates, that have been implicit so far (see also Titelbaum 2022, pp. 208–221).

Suppose we have a predicate language, with the connectives of sentential logic, constant terms, and predicates (leaving quantifiers aside). A very simple language might have a single monadic predicate F, and constants denote successive observations in which F might be observed. Evidence consists in a finite binary sequence indicating the presence or absence of F, and our problem is to figure out what evidence sequences provide support for hypotheses about subsequent observations. An 'inductive method' (Carnap 1955, p. 10) is a procedure for assigning probabilities to hypotheses about the total sequence of outcomes – what Carnap calls a 'state description'. (Every proposition expressible in this language is a Boolean combination of state descriptions.) An example of this sort came up in the previous section, where I noted that a probability assignment that assigns each finite binary A/B sequence of a given length equal probability fails to be inductively rational.

Carnap – and before him, Johnson (1932) – proposed another inductive method than that of the naive POI. A *structure description* is a class of state descriptions which share the same frequencies; that is, they share that structural aspect which is preserved under permutation of outcome order. Carnap opts for this account of structure as particularly appropriate for statistical inference, because such structures preserve frequencies, which are vital for probabilistic theories. In the previous case, as noted in Section 4.3, there are 10 possible structures of the 2^9 possible state descriptions. Carnap's 'method II' says: we ought to be indifferent between structures first, then states (Carnap 1955, pp. 8–14; Zabell 2011, pp. 271–274). Assign equal probability to each structure, then divide that probability equally over each state compatible with a given structure. That gives us the probability distribution in Table 4.

Carnap's m^* can be extended to a full probability function on the space of possibilities c^*. This enables us to evaluate the prior probabilities of hypotheses, as well as conditional probabilities of hypotheses given evidence. The prior probability assigned to 9 Bs is $1/10$; the prior probability assigned to *BBBBBBBBA* is $1/90$. So the probability that the last outcome is a B, given that the 8 preceding outcomes have been Bs, is $1/10/1/10 + 1/90 = 9/10$. Half of all states terminate in a B, so the prior probability is $1/2$; so the observation of 8 Bs strongly supports the hypothesis that the last item will be a B, and confirms it over its initial probability. This method does allow for responsiveness to potential evidence. And it does yield Uniqueness: given a language, purely formal *syntactic* features of state and structure descriptions yield a probability assignment to all hypotheses.

It's bound to be too good to be true. How could syntactic considerations determine a probability assignment over propositions, when the very same proposition can be expressed by sentences with differing syntactic structure? Inconsistency seems unavoidable.

Table 4 Carnap's 'Method II' for determining inductive probability.

Structure	Structure probability	Open state descriptions	State probability m^*
9 As, 0 Bs	1/10	1	1/10
8 As, 1 B	1/10	9	1/90
7 As, 2 Bs	1/10	36	1/360
6 As, 3 Bs	1/10	84	1/840
5 As, 4 Bs	1/10	126	1/1,260
4 As, 5 Bs	1/10	126	1/1,260
3 As, 6 Bs	1/10	84	1/840
2 As, 7 Bs	1/10	36	1/360
1 A, 8 Bs	1/10	9	1/90
0 As, 9 Bs	1/10	1	1/10

Suppose some speakers have introduced a word, 'grue', the usage of which turns out to be best systematised by the following: something is grue iff it is green and examined before 31 December 2030, or blue and not examined before that date (Goodman 1954, chapter 3). At the time of writing, and probably of your reading, everything previously observed is green iff it is grue, so there has been a green/grue regularity in the data so far. If we are to learn from experience in line with Carnap's c^*, we should be confident that green things are grue, and vice versa, going forward. But the first green thing observed on 1 January 2031 will not be grue. So this inductively supported expectation will not be fulfilled.

Carnap's theory cannot accommodate this fact, because the syntactic form of the 'grue' hypotheses and observations is exactly the same as that of the parallel hypotheses and observations including 'green'. 'Grue' was introduced on the basis of a false inductive hypothesis, but having been introduced, it is a fit predicate for use in the construction of state descriptions and structure descriptions, and for the construction of a rational prior. The problem with 'grue' arises once we look at the consequences of applying this syntactic procedure, together with our grasp on the meaning of 'grue'.

To avoid this consequence, we shall have to appeal to some syntactically available feature to exclude 'grue' from our inductive practice. It will be very hard to do so, at least without making unwarranted presumptions about the range of permissible hypotheses (Godfrey-Smith 2003, pp. 578–583). Many things behave differently when observed: people and other social entities, certainly. So there cannot be a general ban of mentioning 'observation' in the hypotheses we consider. Likewise, some data series exhibit discontinuities due to a change in measurement procedure on a certain date; hypotheses that account for the data need to explicitly recognise that date in explaining the slightly different characteristics of the data before and after it. So there cannot be a general ban on mentioning specific dates in hypotheses. 'Grue' is distinctive in including both of these non-forbidden expressions, but we can perhaps see a use case for a similar predicate – for example, when a social science data series changes from using an overt to covert measurement technique, changing the impact of observation on the experimental subjects from a particular date.

The problem with 'grue' isn't intrinsic to the word. The problem is what it *means*. Our background knowledge suggests to us that 'grue' is not a good way of describing reality – it is not a property that captures the structure of how things are. For example, unlike a genuine property, satisfying 'grue' needn't make for genuine resemblance between things which do so (Lewis 1983, p. 345). But this distinction in 'naturalness' between 'green' and 'grue' isn't – cannot be – present in the syntax. The flipside is that any robust theory of confirmation and evidential support will have to make initial presumptions that treat structurally identical claims differently:

> A favoring relation that fails to treat [structurally indistinguishable] identically *plays favorites* among properties. That is, it responds differently to a hypothesis involving one property than it does to a hypothesis that is identical except that it involves a different property. For instance, suppose we have a piece of evidence that mentions greenness and grueness in exactly the same ways, but that evidence favors a hypothesis involving the property of being green over a hypothesis that involves the property of being grue in structurally identical ways. If the evidential favoring relation behaves in this way, it fails to treat predicate permutations identically. And notice that this property favoritism *precedes the influence of the evidence*. It's not that the difference occurs because the evidence indicates that greenness is a property worthy of special consideration; we stipulated that the evidence says exactly the same things about (or using) greenness that it says about (/using) grueness. If we could behold the [evidential favouring] relation itself before any evidence had been plugged in, we could already see that plugging in evidence and hypotheses involving certain properties would cause it to react differently than plugging in evidence and hypotheses that differed only in the properties that appeared. (Titelbaum 2011, pp. 482–483)

4.5 Constructing Priors: Algorithmic Randomness

Carnap's theory is historically important. But it is also of interest because of the rise of digital computation, where many problems thought to be the exclusive province of human intelligence have shown themselves to be amenable to being handled by systems applying syntactic rules of computation. Carnap does not seem himself to have been particularly interested in formulating an inductive algorithm, but the principal intellectual inheritors of his project in computer science have been. Their story is not as well known among philosophers, so I choose it as my final attempt at the explicit construction of a unique prior. It will not be immune to the problems besetting earlier accounts (Sections 4.3, 4.4). I will simplify some of the mathematical details in the interest of accessibility (Eagle 2016; Li & Vitanyi 2008, chapter 2).

Suppose we had some string of sample data about a population and a monadic property F: that the first three items sampled had F, the fourth and fifth lacked it, the sixth has it, and so on: $F, F, F, \neg F, \neg F, F, \neg F, \neg F, \neg F, \neg F, \neg F,$ $F, \neg F, \neg F, F, \ldots$. Or, as a binary sequence: $1, 1, 1, 0, 0, 1, 0, 0, 0, 0, 0, 1, 0,$ $0, 1, \ldots$. The question we face is one of *sequence prediction* (Solomonoff 1964, p. 2): what should we say about the next element in this sequence, given the sample so far? Carnap's preferred method took the frequency of Fs into consideration, the balance of F as against $\neg F$. But it paid no overt attention to the internal structure of the sequence of outcomes.

Laplace observed that, when tossing a coin,

> if heads comes up a hundred times in a row, then this appears to us extraordinary, because the almost infinite number of combinations that can arise in a hundred throws are divided in regular sequences, or those in which we observe a rule that is easy to grasp, and in irregular sequences, that are incomparably more numerous. (Laplace 1995/1825, pp. 16–17)

Laplace notes that an *orderly* sequence is extraordinary if thought to have come about by chance, less extraordinary if it is explicable. As it happens, Carnap's approach respects Laplace's intuition, because it allows orderly data to strongly support orderly hypotheses. The structure descriptions are equiprobable, but there are lots of ways of satisfying the structure 'about half 1s' and only one way of satisfying the structure 'all 1s', so the latter highly orderly sequence gets relatively high probability compared to any one of the many sequences satisfying the former, most of which are random and disorderly.

Carnap has stumbled upon something here: *simplicity*. Orderly sequences obey simple rules; disorderly sequences do not. And since orderly sequences are strongly confirmed by data in agreement with them, we get a preference for simplicity built in to Carnap's inductive methods. But Carnap hasn't latched onto the right mathematical approach. There are still some orderly sequences in the 'about half' structure: $1, 0, 1, 0, 1, 0, \ldots$, for example. This has the frequencies of a disorderly sequence, but isn't disorderly. Carnap's conception is that order is *uniformity*. But in fact, order is exhibited whenever a sequence has a *pattern*. Carnap's framework favours the orderly sequence 'all 1s' over the equally orderly sequence 'alternate 1 and 0'; intuitively, however, that latter pattern is just as indicative of some non-chance theory of the outcomes. This gives the wrong verdict about some straightforward cases. Suppose we'd seen the sequence $0, 1, 0, 1, 0, 1, 0, 1, 0$, and we wonder what comes next. There are slightly more 0s than 1s in the sample data; so c^* slightly favours a prediction of 0 for the next outcome. But the pattern is clear: we ought to predict 1.

A better approach would not overlook regular patterns, including but not limited to uniform outcomes. Solomonoff (1964, p. 3) made a bold proposal: to get a prior that learns from data, assign prior probabilities to sequences that are inversely proportional to how much internal *complexity* they have. A complex sequence doesn't have readily theorised regularities; a simpler sequence is amenable to a theoretical explanation. Solomonoff argues that the best prediction of the next in a sequence of outcomes is that outcome which would make the resulting sequence simpler.[18]

Solomonoff implements his proposal by linking complexity to *compressibility* (Kolmogorov 1963; Li & Vitanyi 2008, pp. 339–370). Fix on a general-purpose computable function f that maps certain binary input sequences to binary output sequences. When $f(\delta) = \sigma$, say that δ is an f-description of σ, or that f decodes δ into its unencoded form σ. A sequence is compressible to the extent that the length of its shortest f-description is considerably shorter than it. This can be used to construct a probability function that favours compressible hypotheses, which is to say, it favours hypotheses that posit orderly structure over those that posit randomness. Where '$|x|$' is the length of x, the f-probability of σ is defined (Rathmanner & Hutter 2011, pp. 1119–1121; Solomonoff 1997, p. 2):

$$\Pr\nolimits_f(\sigma) \stackrel{\text{def}}{=} \sum_{\delta_i \in \{\delta : f(\delta) = \sigma\}} 2^{-|\delta_i|} \approx 2^{-\min\{|\delta| : f(\delta) = \sigma\}}.$$

The f-probability of a sequence is determined by the overall brevity of sequences encoding it, which is dominated by the shortest encoding. The *Kolmogorov complexity* $C_f(\sigma)$ is the length of the shortest input to f encoding σ, so the f-probability of σ is approximately $2^{-C_f(\sigma)}$. Because the probability that a binary sequence of length l is produced by a binary random process is 2^{-l}, we can say that while disorderly sequences, which cannot be compressed, have an algorithmic probability roughly equal to the probability they were produced by chance, orderly sequences have a probability very much greater than the probability they were produced by chance; they are, under this measure over the space of all outcomes, substantially favoured by the prior. But this is still

---

[18] This is a mirror image of the 'best systems' analysis of laws of nature, which proposes that laws are those regularities that most simply and powerfully systematise the pattern of events (Lewis 1994, p. 480).

a probability function, summing to 1 over all hypotheses; this shows the orderly sequences must be very scarce.

There is a potentially troubling dependence on f here, but Kolmogorov (and Solomonoff) show that there is a universal or 'asymptotically optimal' function μ such that

$$\forall f \, \exists k_f \forall \sigma \; C_\mu(\sigma) \leq C_f(\sigma) + k_f.$$

Given that k_f is chosen independently of the sequences, for all sequences beyond a certain length, most decoding functions broadly agree: $C_\mu(\sigma) \approx C_f(\sigma)$.

Algorithmic probability has many desirable qualities. From the perspective of induction, prediction using it can be shown to converge to the 'real' probabilities generating a sequence, in the sense that the distance between the algorithmic posterior probability given the evidence and the real hypothesis converges to zero, so long as the true hypothesis has a non-zero prior (Ortner & Leitgeb 2011, p. 736; Rathmanner & Hutter 2011, pp. 1124–1125; Solomonoff 1997, p. 11). If there is a rule generating the outcomes, the prior bias of algorithmic probability towards hypotheses that invoke a rule to explain a given sequence of outcomes leads the observation of rule-governed outcomes to quickly favour the hypothesis that computably generates those outcomes.

> Early attempts to justify [algorithmic probability] were based on heuristic arguments involving Occam's razor, as well as many examples in which it gave reasonable answers. At the present time, however, we have a much stronger justification than any heuristic argument. [Algorithmic probability] is the only induction technique known to be complete. By this we mean that if there is any describable regularity in a body of data, [algorithmic probability] will discover it using a relatively small sample of the data. (Solomonoff 1997, p. 2)

This result might seem striking. However, Sterkenburg argues that assuming the true hypothesis has a non-zero prior is a very strong assumption, for it requires the true hypothesis to mirror the inductive assumptions that go into constructing the prior. The conditions on the convergence theorem assume, in fact, that the true hypothesis is equivalent to a particular strategy of making predictions on the basis of data, and that the inductive presuppositions about which hypotheses to favour are just the ones it also adopts. Then convergence isn't so surprising: if nature produces outcomes by deploying a function it has induced from the data in the way we would, then our 'discovering' that function by induction is hardly surprising. 'We got out what we put in, after all' (Sterkenburg 2016, p. 476). Moreover, the convergence result might seem in danger of showing too much.

For finite data there is always a regularity, even if the mechanism is completely random. The hypothesis that a sequence lacks inductive regularity is antecedently disfavoured; but surely neutrality between hypotheses requires that we are open to learning a sequence is incompressible?

Even if its justification on the basis of convergence results was too good to be true, perhaps we can still adopt algorithmic probability as a prior because we think the assumption that nature will obey a computable rule is a reasonable one. The theory then promises to turn an inductive assumption about computability into a prior we could deploy.

The first piece of bad news about this idea is that algorithmic probability isn't itself computable; we can't determine how complex a description of the total data is, so we cannot determine what the prior probability of the hypothesis which predicts it with certainty is.[19]

The second piece of bad news is that the robustness of the compressibility results, designed to reassure us that dependence on a particular decoding algorithm was inessential, is in practice a major difficulty. The constant k_f by which each decoder differs from the universal decoder is arbitrarily large – in effect, it may be thought of as instructions telling the universal machine how to pretend to be f. While these instructions may be small in the limit as sequences to be decoded grow arbitrarily, it may completely swamp sequences on the scale we normally treat, so that choice of decoding function will matter a great deal for particular applications. Sterkenburg (2016, pp. 472–474) argues that the choice here is like the choice of prior for the permissive Bayesian – the existence of the universal machine is like the convergence of opinion theorems (Section 4.2), and like them gives no guarantee that the convergence is quick enough for practical use.

> while Solomonoff's framework … may offer a theoretical solution to the problem of induction, it cannot be directly applied to practical problems. (Ortner & Leitgeb 2011, p. 736)

The framework is also subject to more general worries that are at some distance from the technical details. Most obviously, a sequential prediction framework cares only about patterns in the observed data that permit useful compression. The sequence of successive green emeralds is no more or less compressible than the sequence of successive grue emeralds, because only the form of the data

---

[19] Suppose you could compute $C_\mu(\sigma)$: maybe you enumerate all the sequences of length shorter than σ, feed them sequentially into μ, and see if σ pops out. But sometimes μ won't halt on a given input, so this isn't an effective procedure; *for all you know* you have input a short description of σ and are just waiting for an unboundedly long decoding process to conclude. There are computable approximations that converge to Kolmogorov complexity; but the error at each stage of convergence is unknown, so they are not approximate in the normal sense of 'close' (Rissanen 1997; Solomonoff 1997, p. 2).

matters. So if are to avoid inconsistent predictions, some 'green'-favouring constraint must be imposed before applying Solomonoff's recipe. Solomonoff induction, no less than Carnapian inductive methods, satisfy the pre-conditions for generalised language-relativity results (Titelbaum 2011, pp. 482–484). This should temper some of the bolder claims made about the approach, for example, that 'through Solomonoff, ... the problem of formalizing optimal inductive inference is solved' (Rathmanner & Hutter 2011, p. 1078).

Solomonoff himself seems to have come to appreciate this sort of observation, about *grue* and about the prior choice of hypotheses to be considered, and connected it to the practical differences between different universal hypotheses:

> choosing a reference machine we are given the opportunity to insert into the
> *a priori* probability distribution any information about the data that we know
> before we see the data. (Solomonoff 1997, p. 4)

There is another difficulty: how do we turn events distributed across space and time into a sequence of data that can be input to Solomonoff induction?

> Suppose that I am tossing a coin on a train that is moving back and forth on
> tracks that point in a generally easterly direction. . . . Moving from left to right
> (west to east), we see the pattern: HTHTHTHTH . . . . Moving upwards
> (earlier to later), we see the pattern: HHTHHTHHT . . . . Imagine, as we
> can, that these patterns persist forever. What is the limiting relative frequency
> of Heads? Taking the results in their temporal order, the answer is 2/3 . . . .
> But taking them in their west-east spatial order, the answer is 1/2. Now, why
> should one answer have priority over the other? In other words, we have more
> than one limiting relative frequency, depending on which spatio-temporal
> dimension we privilege. (Hájek 2009, pp. 218–219)

If the events are spread out sufficiently over spacetime, there may be no determinate frame-invariant fact about temporal order of outcomes (Maudlin 2012, chapter 5), even if induction is understood as essentially temporal in a way not presumed here. Carnap's maligned C^* does a little better here, at least for finite sequences, because the statistical properties on which he relies are invariant under data permutations. Assumptions about the structure of data must clearly come before one can formulate a space of hypotheses about sequences of data, and is substantively dependent in this example on non-formal views about space and time.

4.6 Conclusion

The upshot, as I see it, of Sections 4.3–4.5 is that substantive philosophical assumptions about prior probabilities are unavoidable. The hope that there is only one rational way to think about evidential support, even though it cannot be articulated in any generally compelling way, starts to look more like an article of faith than a reasonable guess. Technical advances may help us formulate prior assumptions, and distributions derived from maximum entropy or Kolmogorov complexity may well have appealing properties as explications of our preference for neutrality or simplicity. But they cannot function without prior assumptions, and do not let us avoid making them. When the mathematical complexity goes up, and the results start looking more like magic, assumptions are no less present than in the case of permissivism, just slightly better disguised. This lesson generalises well beyond this area of philosophy.

References

Alchourrón, C., Gärdenfors, P., & Makinson, D. (1985). On the logic of theory change: Partial meet contraction and revision functions. *Journal of Symbolic Logic*, **50**, 510–530.

Armendt, B. (1992). Dutch strategies for diachronic rules: When believers see the sure loss coming. In D. Hull, M. Forbes, & K. Okruhlik, eds., vol. 1, East Lansing, MI: Philosophy of Science Association, pp. 217–229.

Armendt, B. (1993). Dutch books, additivity and utility theory. *Philosophical Topics*, **21**(1), 1–20.

Babbage, C. (1827). Notice respecting some errors common to many tables of logarithms. *Memoirs of the Royal Astronomical Society*, **3**, 65–67.

Bacon, F. (2000). *The new organon*. (L. Jardine & M. Silverthorne, eds.), Cambridge University Press. (Original work published 1620)

Baker, V. R. (2009). The channeled scabland: A retrospective. *Annual Review of Earth and Planetary Sciences*, **37**(1), 393–411.

Bradley, D., & Leitgeb, H. (2006). When betting odds and credences come apart: More worries for Dutch book arguments. *Analysis*, **66**(290), 119–127.

Buchak, L. (2013). *Risk and rationality*, Oxford University Press.

Camp, E. (2019). Perspectives and frames in pursuit of ultimate understanding. In S. R. Grimm, ed., *Varieties of understanding: New perspectives from philosophy, psychology, and theology*, New York: Oxford University Press, pp. 17–45.

Carnap, R. (1955). Statistical and inductive probability. In *I. Statistical and inductive probability, II. Inductive logic and science*, Brooklyn, NY: Galois Institute of Mathematics and Art, pp. 1–16.

Carnap, R. (1962). *Logical foundations of probability*, 2nd ed., University of Chicago Press.

Carr, J. R. (2021). Why ideal epistemology? *Mind*, **131**(524), 1131–1162.

Christensen, D. (1999). Measuring confirmation. *Journal of Philosophy*, **96**, 437–461.

Christensen, D. (2004). *Putting logic in its place*, Oxford University Press.

Climenhaga, N. (2024). Epistemic probabilities are degrees of support, not degrees of (rational) belief. *Philosophical and Phenomenological Research*, **108**, 153–176.

Crupi, V. (2021). Confirmation. In E. N. Zalta, ed., *The Stanford encyclopedia of philosophy*, Spring 2021, Metaphysics Research Lab, Stanford: Stanford University. https://plato.stanford.edu/archives/spr2021/entries/confirmation/.

Darwin, C. (1876). *On the origin of species by means of natural selection*, 6th ed., John Murray.

de Finetti, B. (1964). Foresight: Its logical laws, its subjective sources. In H. E. Smokler & H. E. Kyburg Jr, eds., H. E. Kyburg Jr, trans., *Studies in subjective probability*, New York: Wiley, pp. 93–158. (Original work published 1937)

de Finetti, B. (1974). *Theory of probability*. (A. Machí & A. Smith, eds.), vol. 1, Wiley.

Dorling, J. (1979). Bayesian personalism, the methodology of scientific research programmes, and Duhem's problem. *Studies in History and Philosophy of Science*, **10**, 177–187.

Drexel, J. F., Preiss, W. V., & Parker, A. J. (eds.). (2012). *The geology of South Australia*, vol. 1, Adelaide: Government of South Australia. https://sarigba sis.pir.sa.gov.au/WebtopEw/ws/samref/sarig1/image/DDD/BULL054(V1). pdf (Original work published 1993).

Eagle, A. (ed.). (2011). *Philosophy of probability: Contemporary readings*, Routledge.

Eagle, A. (2016). Probability and randomness. In A. Hájek & C. R. Hitchcock, eds., *Oxford handbook of probability and philosophy*, Oxford: Oxford University Press, pp. 440–459.

Earman, J. (1992). *Bayes or bust?*, MIT Press.

Eells, E. & Fitelson, B. (2000). Measuring confirmation and evidence. *Journal of Philosophy*, **97**(12), 663–672.

Eells, E. & Fitelson, B. (2002). Symmetries and asymmetries in evidential support. *Philosophical Studies*, **107**(2), 129–142.

Elga, A. (2007). Reflection and disagreement. *Noûs*, **41**, 478–502.

Feldman, R. (2007). Reasonable religious disagreements. In L. Antony, ed., *Philosophers without gods*, Oxford: Oxford University Press, pp. 194–214.

Fernández, J. (2015). Epistemic generation in memory. *Philosophy and Phenome nological Research*, **92**(3), 620–644.

Fitelson, B. (1999). The plurality of Bayesian measures of confirmation and the problem of measure sensitivity. *Philosophy of Science*, **66**(S3), S362–S378.

Fitelson, B. (2005). Inductive logic. In J. Pfeifer & S. Sarkar, eds., *Philosophy of science: An encyclopedia*, London: Routledge, pp. 384–393.

Fitelson, B. (2006). Logical foundations of evidential support. *Philosophy of Science*, **73**(5), 500–512.

Fitelson, B. (2007). Likelihoodism, Bayesianism, and relational confirmation. *Synthese*, **156**(3), 473–489.

Fitelson, B., & Hájek, A. (2014). Declarations of independence. *Synthese*, **194** (10), 3979–3995.

Fitelson, B. & Hawthorne, J. (2010). How Bayesian confirmation theory handles the paradox of the ravens. In *The place of probability in science*, Netherlands: Springer, pp. 247–275.

Fricker, E. (1995). Telling and trusting: Reductionism and anti-reductionism in the epistemology of testimony. *Mind*, **104**(414), 393–411.

Gaifman, H. (1988). A theory of higher order probability. In B. Skyrms & W. L. Harper, eds., *Causation, chance, and credence*, Dordrecht: Kluwer, pp. 191–219.

Gaifman, H. & Snir, M. (1982). Probabilities over rich languages, testing and randomness. *The Journal of Symbolic Logic*, **47**, 495–548.

Glymour, C. (1981). *Theory and evidence*, University of Chicago Press.

Glynn, L. (2010). A probabilistic analysis of causation. *The British Journal for the Philosophy of Science*, **62**(2), 343–392.

Godfrey-Smith, P. (2003). Goodman's problem and scientific methodology. *Journal of Philosophy*, **100**(11), 573–590.

Gohau, G. (1990). *A history of geology*, Rutgers University Press.

Good, I. J. (1961). The paradox of confirmation (III). *British Journal for the Philosophy of Science*, **11**, 63–64.

Good, I. J. (1967). The white shoe is a red herring. *British Journal for the Philosophy of Science*, **17**(4), 322–322.

Goodman, N. (1954). *Fact, fiction and forecast*, Harvard University Press.

Greco, D., & Hedden, B. (2016). Uniqueness and metaepistemology. *The Journal of Philosophy*, **113**(8), 365–395.

Grice, P. (1989). Logic and conversation. In *Studies in the way of words*, Cambridge MA: Harvard University Press, pp. 22–40.

Hájek, A. (2003). What conditional probability could not be. *Synthese*, **137**(3), 273–323.

Hájek, A. (2008). Dutch book arguments. In P. Anand, P. Pattanaik, & C. Puppe, eds., *Oxford handbook of rational and social choice*, Oxford: Oxford University Press, pp. 173–195.

Hájek, A. (2009). Fifteen arguments against hypothetical frequentism. *Erkenntnis*, **70**(2), 211–235.

Hájek, A. (2011). Triviality pursuit. *Topoi*, **30**(1), 3–15.

Hájek, A., & Hitchcock, C. (2017). Probability for everyone—Even philosophers. In A. Hájek & C. Hitchcock, eds., *Oxford handbook of probability and philosophy*, Oxford: Oxford University Press, pp. 5–30.

Hall, N. (2004). Two mistakes about credence and chance. *Australasian Journal of Philosophy*, **82**, 94–112.

Harman, G. (1965). The inference to the best explanation. *The Philosophical Review*, **74**(1), 88–95.

Harman, G. (1986). *Change in view*, MIT Press.

Hawthorne, J. (2021). Inductive Logic. In E. N. Zalta, ed., *The Stanford encyclopedia of philosophy*, Spring 2021, Metaphysics Research Lab, Stanford: Stanford University.

Hedden, B. (2015). *Reasons without persons*, Oxford University Press.

Hempel, C. G. (1945a). Studies in the logic of confirmation I. *Mind*, **54**(213), 1–26.

Hempel, C. G. (1945b). Studies in the logic of confirmation II. *Mind*, **54**(214), 97–121.

Henderson, L. (2014). Bayesianism and inference to the best explanation. *The British Journal for the Philosophy of Science*, **65**(4), 687–715.

Henderson, L. (2022). The problem of induction. In E. N. Zalta & U. Nodelman, eds., *The Stanford encyclopedia of philosophy*, Stanford: Metaphysics Research Lab, Stanford University.

Hendrick, R. E. & Helvie, M. A. (2011). United States preventive services task force screening mammography recommendations: Science ignored. *American Journal of Roentgenology*, **196**(2), W112–W116.

Horowitz, S. (2014). Immoderately rational. *Philosophical Studies*, **167**(1), 41–56.

Horwich, P. (1982). *Probability and evidence*, Cambridge University Press.

Hosiasson-Lindenbaum, J. (1940). On confirmation. *Journal of Symbolic Logic*, **5**, 133–148.

Howson, C. (1991). The "old evidence" problem. *British Journal for the Philosophy of Science*, **42**, 547–555.

Howson, C. (2000). *Hume's problem: Induction and the justification of belief*, Oxford University Press.

Howson, C. & Urbach, P. (1993). *Scientific reasoning: The Bayesian approach*, 2nd ed., Open Court.

Hume, D. (1999). *An enquiry concerning human understanding*. (T. L. Beauchamp, ed.), Oxford University Press. (Original work published 1748)

Hume, D. (2000). *A treatise of human nature*. (D. F. Norton & M. J. Norton, eds.), Oxford University Press. (Original work published 1739)

Ismael, J. (2008). Raid! Dissolving the big, bad bug. *Noûs*, **42**(2), 292–307.

Jackson, E. (2019). How belief-credence dualism explains away pragmatic encroachment. *Philosophical Quarterly*, **69**, 511–533.

Jaynes, E. T. (1957). Information theory and statistical mechanics. *Physical Review*, **106**(4), 620–630.

Jaynes, E. T. (1968). Prior probabilities. *IEEE Transactions on Systems Science and Cybernetics*, **4**(3), 227–241.

Jeffrey, R. C. (1983a). Bayesianism with a human face. In J. Earman, ed., *Testing scientific theories*, vol. X, Minneapolis, MN: University of Minnesota Press, pp. 133–156.

Jeffrey, R. C. (1983b). *The logic of decision*, University of Chicago Press.

Jeffrey, R. C. (1992). Probability and the art of judgment. In *Probability and the art of judgment*, Cambridge: Cambridge University Press, pp. 44–76.

Jeffrey, R. C. (2008). *Subjective probability: The real thing*, Cambridge University Press.

Jevons, W. S. (1874). *The principles of science*, vol. 1, London: Macmillan.

Johnson, W. E. (1932). Probability: The deductive and inductive problems. *Mind*, **41**(164), 409–423.

Joyce, J. M. (1998). A nonpragmatic vindication of probabilism. *Philosophy of Science*, **65**(4), 575–603.

Joyce, J. M. (2007). Epistemic deference: The case of chance. *Proceedings of the Aristotelian Society (Hardback)*, **107**(1pt2), 187–206.

Kahneman, D. & Tversky, A. (1979). Prospect theory: An analysis of decision under risk. *Econometrica*, **47**(2), 263.

Kelly, K. T. & Glymour, C. (2004). Why probability does not capture the logic of scientific confirmation. In C. Hitchcock, ed., *Contemporary debates in philosophy of science*, Oxford: Blackwell, pp. 94–114.

Kemeny, J. G. (1955). Fair bets and inductive probabilities. *Journal of Symbolic Logic*, **20**, 263–273.

Keynes, J. M. (1921). *A treatise on probability*, Macmillan.

Kim, B. (2017). Pragmatic encroachment in epistemology. *Philosophy Compass*, **12**(5), e12415: 1–14.

Koester, R. J. (2008). *Lost person behaviour*, dbS Productions.

Kolmogorov, A. N. (1956). *Foundations of the theory of probability*. (N. Morrison, ed. & trans.), 2nd ed., Chelsea. (Original work published 1933)

Kolmogorov, A. N. (1963). On tables of random numbers. *Sankhyā*, **25**, 369–376.

Konek, J. (2019). Comparative probabilities. In R. Pettigrew & J. Weisberg, eds., *The open handbook of formal epistemology*, London, Ontario: PhilPapers Foundation, pp. 267–348.

Koopman, B. O. (1940). The axioms and algebra of intuitive probability. *The Annals of Mathematics*, **41**(2), 269.

Kopec, M. & Titelbaum, M. G. (2016). The uniqueness thesis. *Philosophy Compass*, **11**(4), 189–200.

Kotzen, M. (2012). Dragging and confirming. *The Philosophical Review*, **121** (1), 55–93.

Kyburg, J. & Henry E. (1978). Subjective probability: Criticisms, reflections, and problems. *Journal of Philosophical Logic*, **7**, 157–180.

Kyburg, J. & Henry E. (1983). *Epistemology and inference*, University of Minnesota Press.

Lackey, J. (2005). Memory as a generative epistemic source. *Philosophy and Phenomenological Research*, **70**, 636–658.

Lackey, J. (2008). *Learning from words: Testimony as a source of knowledge*, Oxford University Press.

Laplace, P.-S. (1995). *Philosophical essay on probabilities*. (A. I. Dale, trans.), 5th ed., Springer. https://doi.org/10.1007/978-1-4612-4184-3 (Original work published 1825).

Lehman, C. D., Arao, R. F., Sprague, B. L. et al. (2017). National performance benchmarks for modern screening digital mammography: Update from the breast cancer surveillance consortium. *Radiology*, **283**(1), 49–58.

Lehman, R. S. (1955). On confirmation and rational betting. *Journal of Symbolic Logic*, **20**, 251–262.

Lewis, D. (1976). Probabilities of conditionals and conditional probabilities. *Philosophical Review*, **85**(3), 297–315.

Lewis, D. (1979). Scorekeeping in a language game. *Journal of Philosophical Logic*, **8**(1), 339–359.

Lewis, D. (1983). New work for a theory of universals. *Australasian Journal of Philosophy*, **61**(4), 343–377.

Lewis, D. (1986a). A subjectivist's guide to objective chance. In *Philosophical papers*, vol. 2, Oxford: Oxford University Press, pp. 83–132.

Lewis, D. (1986b). Causal explanation. In *Philosophical papers*, vol. 2, Oxford: Oxford University Press, pp. 214–240.

Lewis, D. (1994). Humean supervenience debugged. In *Papers in metaphysics and epistemology*, Cambridge: Cambridge University Press, pp. 224–246.

Lewis, D. (1996). Elusive knowledge. *Australasian Journal of Philosophy*, **74**(4), 549–567.

Lewis, D. (1999). Why conditionalize? In *Papers in metaphysics and epistemology*, Cambridge: Cambridge University Press, pp. 403–407.

Li, M. & Vitanyi, P. M. B. (2008). *An introduction to Kolmogorov complexity and its applications*, New York: Springer Verlag. https://doi.org/10.1007/978-0-387-49820-1.

Lipton, P. (2004). *Inference to the best explanation*, 2nd ed., Routledge.

Lyell, C. (1830). *Principles of geology*, vol. 1, London: James Murray.

Maher, P. (1993). *Betting on theories*, Cambridge University Press.

Maher, P. (1996). Subjective and objective confirmation. *Philosophy of Science*, **63**, 149–174.

Maher, P. (1997). Depragmatized Dutch book arguments. *Philosophy of Science*, **64**, 291–305.

Maudlin, T. (2012). *Philosophy of physics: Space and time*, Princeton University Press.

Meacham, C. J. G. (2014). Impermissive Bayesianism. *Erkenntnis*, **79**(S6), 1185–1217.

Meacham, C. J. G. (2016). Ur-priors, conditionalization, and ur-prior condition-alization. *Ergo*, **3**(17), 444–492.

Meacham, C. J. G. (2019). Deference and uniqueness. *Philosophical Studies*, **176**(3), 709–732.

Meacham, C. J. G. & Weisberg, J. (2011). Representation theorems and the foundations of decision theory. *Australasian Journal of Philosophy*, **89**(4), 641–663.

Milne, P. (1983). A note on scale invariance. *British Journal for the Philosophy of Science*, **34**, 49–55.

Milne, P. (1996). $\log[P(h|eb)/P(h|b)]$ is the one true measure of confirmation. *Philosophy of Science*, **63**, 21–26.

Moretti, L. (2003). Why the converse consequence condition cannot be accepted. *Analysis*, **63**(280), 297–300.

Neth, S. (2025). Better foundations for subjective probability. *Australasian Journal of Philosophy*. https://doi.org/10.1080/00048402.2024.2329970.

Norton, J. D. (2003). A material theory of induction. *Philosophy of Science*, **70** (4), 647–670.

Norton, J. D. (2011). Challenges to Bayesian confirmation theory. In P. S. Bandyopadhyay & M. R. Forster, eds., *Handbook of the philosophy of science: Philosophy of statistics*, vol. 7, Amsterdam: North-Holland, pp. 391–439.

Ortner, R. & Leitgeb, H. (2011). Mechanizing induction. In D. M. Gabbay, S. Hartmann, & J. Woods, eds., *Handbook of the history of logic: Inductive logic*, vol. 10, Amsterdam: North-Holland, pp. 719–772.

Paul, L. A. (2014). *Transformative experience*, Oxford University Press.

Pettigrew, R. (2016). *Accuracy and the laws of credence*, Oxford University Press.

Pettigrew, R. (2020a). *Choosing for changing selves*, Oxford: Oxford University Press.

Pettigrew, R. (2020b). *Dutch book arguments*, Cambridge University Press. https://doi.org/10.1017/9781108581813.

Popper, K. (1959). *The logic of scientific discovery*, Hutchinson.

Pryor, J. (2000). The skeptic and the dogmatist. *Noûs*, **34**(4), 517–549.

Ramsey, F. P. (1990). Truth and probability. In D. H. Mellor, ed., *Philosophical papers*, Cambridge: Cambridge University Press, pp. 52–94. (Original work published 1926)

Rathmanner, S. & Hutter, M. (2011). A philosophical treatise of universal induction. *Entropy*, **13**(6), 1076–1136.

Rissanen, J. (1997). Stochastic complexity in learning. *Journal of Computer and System Sciences*, **55**(1), 89–95.

Rosen, D. A. (1978). In defense of a probabilistic theory of causality. *Philosophy of Science*, **45**(4), 604–613.

Rosen, G. (2001). Nominalism, naturalism, epistemic relativism. *Philosophical Perspectives*, **15**, 60–91.

Rosenkrantz, R. D. (1977). *Inference, method and decision: Towards a Bayesian philosophy of science*, Dordrecht: D. Reidel.

Royall, R. M. (1997). *Statistical evidence: A likelihood paradigm*, Hall.

Savage, L. J. (1954). *The foundations of statistics*, Wiley.

Savage, L. J. (1972). *The foundations of statistics*, 2nd ed., Wiley.

Schick, F. (1986). Dutch bookies and money pumps. *Journal of Philosophy*, **83**, 112–119.

Schlesinger, G. N. (1995). Measuring degrees of confirmation. *Analysis*, **55**, 208–212.

Schoenfield, M. (2012). Permission to believe: Why permissivism is true and what it tells us about irrelevant influences on belief. *Noûs*, **48**(2), 193–218.

Schupbach, J. N. (2022). *Bayesianism and scientific reasoning*, Cambridge University Press. https://doi.org/10.1017/9781108657563.

Seidenfeld, T. (1986). Entropy and uncertainty. *Philosophy of Science*, **53**, 467–491.

Shackel, N. & Rowbottom, D. P. (2020). Bertrand's paradox and the maximum entropy principle. *Philosophy and Phenomenological Research*, **101**(3), 505–523.

Shogenji, T. (2003). A condition for transitivity in probabilistic support. *The British Journal for the Philosophy of Science*, **54**(4), 613–616.

Skyrms, B. (1984). *Pragmatics and empiricism*, Yale University Press.

Skyrms, B. (1987). Coherence. In N. Rescher, ed., *Scientific inquiry in philosophical perspective*, Pittsburgh, PA: University of Pittsburgh Press, pp. 225–242.

Sober, E. (1994). Contrastive empiricism. In *From a biological point of view: Essays in evolutionary philosophy*, Cambridge: Cambridge University Press, pp. 114–135.

Solomonoff, R. (1964). A formal theory of inductive inference, part I. *Information and Control*, **7**, 1–22.

Solomonoff, R. (1997). *Does algorithmic probability solve the problem of induction?* http://world.std.com/~rjs/isis96.pdf.

Staffel, J. (2020). *Unsettled thoughts: A theory of degrees of rationality*, Oxford University Press.

Stalnaker, R. C. (1973). Presuppositions. *Journal of Philosophical Logic*, **2**, 447–457.

Stalnaker, R. C. (1984). *Inquiry*, MIT Press.

Stalnaker, R. C. (1999). On the representation of context. In *Context and content*, Oxford: Oxford University Press, pp. 96–113. (Original work published 1998)

Stanley, J. (2000). Context and logical form. *Linguistics and Philosophy*, **23**(4), 391–434.

Stanley, J. & Szabó, Z. G. (2000). On quantifier domain restriction. *Mind and Language*, **15**(2–3), 219–261.

Steel, D. (1996). Bayesianism and the value of diverse evidence. *Philosophy of Science*, **63**, 666–674.

Stefánsson, H. O. (2017). What is "real" in probabilism? *Australasian Journal of Philosophy*, **95**(3), 573–587.

Sterkenburg, T. F. (2016). Solomonoff prediction and Occam's razor. *Philosophy of Science*, **83**(4), 459–479.

Straßer, C. (forthcoming). *Non-monotonic logic*, Cambridge University Press.

Strevens, M. (2001). The Bayesian treatment of auxiliary hypotheses. *British Journal for the Philosophy of Science*, **52**, 515–537.

Strevens, M. (2004). Bayesian confirmation theory: Inductive logic, or mere inductive framework? *Synthese*, **141**(3), 365–379.

Strevens, M. (2006). Notes on Bayesian confirmation theory. www.nyu.edu/gsas/dept/philo/user/strevens/Classes/Conf06/BCT.pdf.

Swinburne, R. (1971). The paradoxes of confirmation: A survey. *American Philosophical Quarterly*, **8**(4), 318–330.

Talbott, W. J. (1991). Two principles of Bayesian epistemology. *Philosophical Studies*, **62**(2), 135–150.

Titelbaum, M. G. (2011). Not enough there there: evidence, reasons, and language independence. *Philosophical Perspectives*, **24**(1), 477–528.

Titelbaum, M. G. (2022). *Fundamentals of Bayesian epistemology*, vol. 1, Oxford University Press.

van Fraassen, B. C. (1980). *The scientific image*, Clarendon Press. https://doi.org/10.1093/0198244274.001.0001.

van Fraassen, B. C. (1989). *Laws and symmetry*, Oxford University Press.

Weisberg, J. (2009). Commutativity or holism? A dilemma for conditionalizers. *The British Journal for the Philosophy of Science*, **60**(4), 793–812.

Weisberg, J. (2011). Varieties of Bayesianism. In D. Gabbay, S. Hartmann, & J. Woods, eds., *Handbook of the history of logic: Inductive logic*, vol. 10, Amsterdam: North-Holland, pp. 477–551.

White, R. (2005). Epistemic permissiveness. *Philosophical Perspectives*, **19**, 445–459.

White, R. (2009). Evidential symmetry and mushy credence. In T. S. Gendler & J. Hawthorne, eds., *Oxford studies in epistemology*, vol. 3, Oxford: Oxford University Press, pp. 161–186.

Williams, J. R. G. (2016). Probability and nonclassical logic. In C. R. Hitchcock & A. Hájek, eds., *The Oxford handbook of probability and philosophy*, Oxford: Oxford University Press, pp. 248–276.

Williamson, J. (2011). An objective Bayesian account of confirmation. In D. Dieks, W. J. Gonzalez, S. Hartmann, T. Uebel, & M. Weber, eds., *Explanation, prediction, and confirmation*, vol. 2, Dordrecht: Springer, pp. 53–81.

Williamson, T. (2000). *Knowledge and its limits*, Oxford University Press.

Zabell, S. L. (2011). Carnap and the logic of inductive inference. In D. M. Gabbay, S. Hartmann, & J. Woods, eds., *Handbook of the history of logic: Inductive logic*, vol. 10, Amsterdam: North-Holland, pp. 265–309.

Zalabardo, J. (2009). An argument for the likelihood-ratio measure of confirmation. *Analysis*, **69**(4), 630–635.

Acknowledgements

I am grateful for the forbearance and advice of the series editors as I worked to complete this Element, to an anonymous reviewer for constructive comments, to Lizzie Maughan and Atheer Al-Khalfa for comments on the near-final manuscript, and to Marshall Abrams for facilitating a 2022 PSA symposium on randomness where a version of Section 4.5 was presented. Some of the work on this Element was supported by a grant from the Australian Research Council under its Discovery Projects scheme (DP200100190).

Cambridge Elements ≡

Philosophy and Logic

Bradley Armour-Garb
SUNY Albany

Bradley Armour-Garb is chair and Professor of Philosophy at SUNY Albany. His books include *The Law of Non-Contradiction* (co-edited with Graham Priest and J. C. Beall, 2004), *Deflationary Truth* and *Deflationism and Paradox* (both co-edited with J. C. Beall, 2005), *Pretense and Pathology* (with James Woodbridge, Cambridge University Press, 2015), *Reflections on the Liar* (2017), and *Fictionalism in Philosophy* (co-edited with Fred Kroon, 2020).

Frederick Kroon
The University of Auckland

Frederick Kroon is Emeritus Professor of Philosophy at the University of Auckland. He has authored numerous papers in formal and philosophical logic, ethics, philosophy of language, and metaphysics, and is the author of *A Critical Introduction to Fictionalism* (with Stuart Brock and Jonathan McKeown-Green, 2018).

About the Series

This Cambridge Elements series provides an extensive overview of the many and varied connections between philosophy and logic. Distinguished authors provide an up-to-date summary of the results of current research in their fields and give their own take on what they believe are the most significant debates influencing research, drawing original conclusions.

Cambridge Elements ☰

Philosophy and Logic

A full series listing is available at: www.cambridge.org/EPL

Printed in the United States
by Baker & Taylor Publisher Services